THE GOOD RUSSIAN

THE GOOD RUSSIAN

In Search of a Nation's Soul

JANA BAKUNINA

The
Bridge
Street
Press

THE BRIDGE STREET PRESS

First published in Great Britain in 2025 by the Bridge Street Press

1 3 5 7 9 10 8 6 4 2

A CIP catalogue record for this book
is available from the British Library.

Hardback ISBN 978-0-349-13658-5
Trade paperback ISBN 978-0-349-13659-2

Typeset in EB Garamond by M Rules
Printed and bound in Great Britain by
Clays Ltd, Elcograf S.p.A.

Papers used by The Bridge Street Press are from well-managed forests
and other responsible sources.

FSC
www.fsc.org

MIX
Paper | Supporting
responsible forestry
FSC® C104740

The Bridge Street Press
An imprint of
Little, Brown Book Group
Carmelite House
50 Victoria Embankment
London EC4Y 0DZ

The authorised representative
in the EEA is
Hachette Ireland
8 Castlecourt Centre
Dublin 15, D15 XTP3, Ireland
(email: info@hbgi.ie)

An Hachette UK Company
www.hachette.co.uk

www.littlebrown.co.uk

In memory of my grandfather –
what would he have made of it all?

Since February, we have been living in a black-and-white world, in which you are either on one side or the other.

LEV RUBINSTEIN (1947–2024)

Contents

Author's Note

I have changed many names and identifying details, including occupations, backgrounds, family members and settings, to respect the privacy and protect the safety of those I have spoken to, without compromising the integrity of the story. I have reconstructed conversations to the best of my ability, evoking the essence and spirit of what was said to me.

Chapter 1

'What Is the Purpose of your Visit?'

T he border control officer appears to be in his early twenties and inspects my Russian passport through thick glasses. His mother must feel relieved for him – his job at a provincial border control office, a branch of the Federal Security Service, and his severe myopia keep him safe from the war in Ukraine. He looks up and asks to see my British passport. I comply with his request. I even smile. He pauses for a moment, taken aback by my friendliness, then peers at his computer. I've been through this before.

A year earlier, in September 2022, I had travelled to Russia for the first time since the full-scale invasion began that February to look after my mother, who had fallen and fractured her sacrum. Without direct flights to Russia from Europe, I flew to Tallinn and then took a bus to Narva, a town with a striking backdrop: two medieval castles standing sentinel on opposite sides of the river that separates Estonia from Russia. It was at the Narva border control office where I was first asked to surrender my British passport and smartphone before being photographed, fingerprinted and interviewed by two plain-clothed Federal Security Service officers. At the time, I struggled to stay composed. While the officers remained courteous, they never explained why I had been singled out. It was only during questioning that they revealed what made me 'special': 'You are a citizen of a non-friendly state.' Having had dual British and Russian citizenship for over a decade, I had already been asked, 'Are you a spy?' and 'Do you know anyone at MI6?' 'Not that I know,' I replied. 'But spies? They could be anywhere.' They released me, promising another 'chat' the next time I travelled to Russia. I remember leaving the building with the heaviness of a cartoon convict, dragging a ball and chain. Nothing truly grave happened, but I felt exhausted.

This time in October 2023, I had decided to fly from Turkey directly to Yekaterinburg, where I grew up. Yekaterinburg, Russia's fourth-largest city of some 1.5 million people, is situated in the Ural Mountains, which divide Western Russia and Siberia. It takes a two-hour flight or twenty hours on a fast train to travel there from Moscow. Famously, it is also where Tsar Nikolai II and his family were kept under house arrest and then executed by Bolsheviks in July 1918.

I grew up in a middle-class family of civil servants and academics. During perestroika, my father turned to entrepreneurship, initially importing microscopes and other lab equipment from Germany. At school, I learned English and later German, eager to study abroad and take advantage of the openness of the 1990s. After two years at a boarding school in Germany where, thanks

to my father's efforts, I received a full scholarship, I came back
to Yekaterinburg in the summer of 1998. The city was thriving,
with many foreign companies opening offices and showrooms,
and Western financiers coming in to meet local aluminium and
copper magnates and pour money into the rapidly transforming
Russian economy. But that summer, Russia defaulted on its foreign and domestic debt, which led to a financial crisis. My father's
firm, like many small businesses, was nearly wiped out by the de-
valuation of the ruble. This painful personal experience, coupled
with government ineptitude, only strengthened my resolve to
leave Russia. I was eighteen years old and with a place at Oxford.
I left a year later – just before Putin took over my country – and
have lived in the UK ever since.

In the two decades that followed, I have never doubted my
Russianness. It stayed with me when I was able to draw on my
lived experience under Soviet rule when participating in debates
on whether socialism would work in the West. As a Russian, I
feel proud of my numeracy, a skill strangely disdained by some
Brits. My heritage instilled in me the work ethic that earned me
a first-class degree at Oxford and a career in banking. Perhaps
it was the intellectual haughtiness of someone brought up on
Pushkin, Chekhov and Tolstoy that gave me the confidence to
turn from finance to writing. I grew up believing in the proudly
multi-ethnic country that had established the periodic table,
sent the first man into space and defeated fascism. I had to re-
examine how I thought about Russia in relation to the former
Soviet Republics and get other perspectives on the Second
World War. While I had to rethink what I'd imbibed during
my Soviet childhood, I never betrayed my nationality. I call
London my home, but Russia – with all its maddening contra-
dictions – is where I came from. I used to think of it as a place

I could always return to, like a sailor occasionally dreaming of their homeland.

Hence, when the bespectacled officer enquires about the purpose of my visit, it stirs something within me. I remain a Russian citizen; do I need a reason to return? To the officer, I reply, 'I am visiting my family.' This is true enough. But I'm also here to ask questions and seek understanding. This I keep to myself. He returns my passports and waves me through. Relief.

The questions began percolating on that fateful morning of 24 February 2022.

The day before, the *Evening Standard* had got in touch, asking if I wanted to write a comment piece about the massed Russian troops at the eastern border of Ukraine. I interviewed a few people in Russia and, later that evening, called my friend Sergiy in Kyiv. He was in a bar. I could hear music and buzzing voices in the background. 'We don't know what's happening, but hey, life goes on,' he said. We chatted for a bit longer, and I called it a night. In the morning, I woke up to a different world – one where Russians invade, kill, loot and pretend it's some swift, trivial 'special operation'. I was stunned. Furious, ashamed, but most of all helpless. The article had to be rewritten. That is what pulled me out of my stupor. It was difficult to find words to express the anger I felt.

The day after the invasion, I was sitting in my therapist's office. She was about my age, kind and lively, her sleeves rolled up. I told her about my background and how I was finding it difficult to talk to anyone about what was happening. As a Russian, I was proud of the sacrifice my ancestors had made to defeat Hitler in the Second World War. As a child, I believed in 'Never again' and grew up a pacifist. How was it possible that the same nation that had saved the world from Nazism was now the aggressor? How could our president be compared to Hitler?

I told my therapist that my friends in London didn't seem to know what to say. I didn't blame them. I told her I could not speak to my father, who thought me a traitor for living in the West and taking Ukraine's side ever since Russia annexed Crimea in 2014 and sent mercenaries to fuel separatism in Eastern Ukraine. When I talked to my mother, the person I am closest to, I stumbled. It was an open wound. I had called her the day before expecting to engage in mutual outrage. Instead, my mother was silent. She did not believe Russia had invaded Ukraine. 'It was just a "Special Military Operation",' she said. 'We are firing missiles at Kyiv,' I pointed out. 'I've seen photos and videos, and I spoke to Sergiy – you once met in Hyde Park?' I tried to open her eyes but only succeeded in making her upset. She said I was frightening her with my 'aggression', a word I recognised from the Kremlin's rhetoric. 'It's Western aggression,' they'd say again and again, defending their actions in Syria or explaining pro-EU demonstrations in Ukraine in 2013 or even post-2020 presidential election protests in Belarus. In any case, my mother didn't want to talk to me 'about that'.

'About that' meant Putin tightening his authoritarian control; it meant the assassination of opposition politicians; the fabulous wealth of Putin's men; corruption and theft; the closing down of independent media outlets and NGOs; Russia's meddling in Syria and African countries like Mali and Burkina Faso; and the endless anti-Western propaganda on TV and online. My mother didn't want to hear any of that. Hoping to preserve a relationship with at least one of my parents, I rarely brought those things up. Had I been wrong not to challenge her sooner? In the days after the invasion, we simply could not speak to each other. We both cried, but not together.

The therapist listened to me and sat very still. Looking at

the clock in the room, I asked if it was time. She pressed her lips together and stood up. Her eyes were moist. I thanked her and left. That night I sent a message to my mother saying that I loved her. The next morning, I went to an anti-war protest in Westminster.

If I was a little nervous about joining Ukrainians who would be making it very clear how they felt about Russia, I was soon swept away by the community of like-minded people carrying placards like 'I'm Russian and I'm Ashamed', 'Hands Off Ukraine' and 'Stop Putin'. Here I found Russians and Ukrainians huddling together with deep bags under their eyes; Russians who found it impossible to talk to their parents back home; and Kazakhs, Georgians and Estonians who had come out in solidarity. We hugged and exchanged contact details. We also shared stories about Russians who had lived in London for years and yet still staunchly supported Putin. We all hoped that they would finally question their allegiance. Few of them did. One 'Russian mums' neighbourhood WhatsApp group became flooded with xeno-phobic memes and calls for 'the necessary measures to purify Ukraine'. I couldn't even begin to process the hatred.

Meanwhile, speaking out in Russia, already very difficult and mostly illegal after two decades of legislation, became downright impossible. Anyone peacefully demonstrating with a sign read-ing 'No to War' was arrested. Most were beaten up and detained for fifteen days. One Moscow friend who wanted to protest against the invasion told me that she was still breastfeeding her son and did not want to risk arrest. Within ten days of invading Ukraine, the Russian Duma adopted new laws criminalising independent war reporting and 'discrediting' or 'spreading fake news' about the Russian Armed Forces, whether by protest or social media post. Calling for an end to the war – or even using the word 'war' – became punishable by up to fifteen years in prison. Some 150 journalists left Russia within a fortnight.

A friend told me to book a holiday. It seemed a strange idea. Weren't people fleeing Ukraine, leaving Russia, raising money to support refugees, signing up to take in Ukrainian families, protesting the war outside Russian embassies in every major capital city? In truth, many Russians I knew had succumbed to a similar state of inertia. So many had stopped talking to their families in Russia, unable to reconcile the horror of seeing wounded people and destroyed buildings in Ukraine with their Russian counterparts' denial that anything tragic was happening. I turned to German post-war literature, like Bernhard Schlink's *The Reader*, seeking to soak myself in remorse. But I got distracted by the news. In April 2022, a prominent Kremlin critic, Vladimir Kara-Murza, left his family in the US and travelled to Moscow to speak out in public against the invasion. He was arrested immediately. A thirty-two-year-old artist, Sasha Skochilenko, was arrested in St. Petersburg for replacing a handful of supermarket price tags with messages criticising Russia's invasion of Ukraine. 'Stop the war! In the first three days, 4,300 Russian soldiers were killed. Why don't they show it on TV?' said one tag. 'Russian forces have destroyed 80 per cent of Mariupol. For what?' said another. A year later, Kara-Murza, despite or because of his dual Russian-British citizenship, was sentenced to twenty-five years in a penal colony, charged with 'high treason' for 'disseminating knowingly false information about the Russian Armed Forces'. In November 2023, Skochilenko was sentenced to seven years, a maximum sentence. Fortunately, both of them were released as part of a prisoner exchange on 1 August 2024.

My friend was right: I needed to get away. I went to Ischia, then stayed a few more days on the Amalfi Coast. In Positano, I ordered a coffee in a small cafe and overheard a barista speaking to a waiter in Russian with a Ukrainian accent. I said how sorry I was for what was happening. The barista replied that it wasn't my fault. Then she told me that she'd come from Mariupol, where she had worked as a florist. I immediately pictured the city, which had come under siege by Russian forces at the end of February 2022. Mariupol's hospitals and vital infrastructure had been destroyed, depriving its citizens of electricity and drinking water. A theatre, clearly marked as a refuge for children, was struck by missiles. Civilians were denied the chance to escape or access humanitarian aid. The young woman in the cafe was lucky. She escaped and got in touch with a friend who had moved to Positano some years ago. She was able to stay with him and get a job first at a laundry and then at this cafe. She was happier working here as it wasn't so lonely. 'Tell me,' she said, 'did you make it to Pompeii? It's a must!' I nodded, touched by her humanity. Then she followed up: 'Do Russians know what is really happening to us? How can they support it?'

These questions kept piling up. Unlike in the Soviet days, full media censorship is no longer possible in the twenty-first century. From the conversations with my family and friends, I know that while my mother only watches TV and reads Yandex, the Russian social media portal, on her smartphone, both editorially controlled by the government, many others use VPNs to access banned media sources and subscribe to various broadcast channels on Telegram. My mother too has access to Telegram and, like everyone, chooses what she consumes.

Information still flows into Russia, but getting information out is a problem. A lack of impartial opinion surveys means it is impossible to say how many Russians actually support the regime and its military aggression. Understanding their views is even trickier when there are almost no Western or independent journalists left in the country – some left, some were expelled and some ended up in jail. In March 2023, *Wall Street Journal* reporter Evan Gershkovich was arrested in Yekaterinburg and taken to a prison in Moscow accused of espionage, a charge he, his employer and the US government vehemently denied. In July 2024, he was sentenced to sixteen years in prison before his release as part of the prisoner swap. In October 2023, Alsu Kurmasheva, a dual Russian and US citizen who worked for Radio Free Europe/Radio Liberty, was arrested in Kazan when visiting her family for failing to register as a 'foreign agent'. In July 2024, she was sentenced to six and a half years for spreading 'false information' about the Russian army. Fortunately, she too was released on 1 August 2024. Some thirty Russian journalists, including Antonina Favorskaya, Sergei Karelin, Konstantin Gabov and Artem Kriger, remain behind bars.

Without direct access, the Western media often reports on Russians as 'them' – fervent supporters of Putin in the majority and just a handful of brave anti-government activists in opposition. I found myself thinking of the many successful middle-aged Russians I know who consider themselves well-informed, yet genuinely proud of Russia and its foreign policy. I also know people who struggle to breathe in Russia today. Some have left and others have stayed, both groups forced to make all sorts of compromises with the regime and with themselves. These are ordinary people I grew up with in Yekaterinburg. I hated the idea of these individuals being referred to as one homogenous 'them'.

When I decided to go back to Russia in autumn 2023, I already had an idea that people of different political persuasions had retained their views following the full-scale invasion of Ukraine. Putin supporters had rallied behind him and his

'Special Military Operation'; those of his opponents who stayed in Russia had to find a way to adapt to significantly curtailed freedoms. Following local news remotely, watching clips of the Russian TV programmes now banned in the West, reading the press and social media posts covering Russia and speaking to friends in Moscow and Yekaterinburg, I could piece together a patchwork of what it was like to live in Russia. But I sensed that a complete picture would be altogether different. A year earlier, in 2022, while visiting my mother as she recovered from her fracture, I had stayed with her in the countryside and resisted going into town or seeing friends. This time I prepared to immerse myself in Russian life and absorb as much as I could in person. I resolved to listen rather than to argue; seeking to understand rather than question. I also wanted to give a voice to people who are not represented in the Western media: ordinary people who neither speak for the Kremlin nor speak out against the regime in public. How has the war affected their lives, and how do they see the future? Is Russia inexorably trending back towards totalitarianism? Is there any hope of turning that around? What do my friends in Russia think of the West, and can we ever reconcile our diverging views? And what about my own family? Like many other Russian expats, I had stopped talking to my parents about politics because I felt it was futile. Could I at least attempt to understand them?

Chapter 2

Doublethink

In 2021, my cousin, who lives in Moscow, sent me some of his late mother's letters that he had typed up during lockdown. In a letter from April 1989, my aunt writes about George Orwell's *Nineteen Eighty-Four*, which she had started reading in the Soviet literary magazine *New World* after the novel's ban had been lifted. She thinks the book is about Stalinist times. 'It's interesting,' she remarks, 'but what concerns me right now is how to survive without soap.' She explains that soap has disappeared from the shelves, and she has spent half a day after work running from one store to the next trying to find it. 'What price are we paying for all of this? Reduced to trying to score basic groceries, our lives have become primitive and ugly. Our way of life [in the USSR] is demeaning, and it cripples our souls.'

Perhaps my aunt felt that *Nineteen Eighty-Four* was too harsh a comparison to her own life in the Soviet Union. Born under Stalin, she grew up with Khrushchev and Brezhnev and studied medicine to become a brilliant cardiologist. During perestroika and glasnost, like any Soviet citizen, she was frustrated with the ineffectiveness of Gorbachev's reforms and the shortages but delighted by the openness that allowed her to read George Orwell, Vasily Grossman and Aleksandr Solzhenitsyn. Had she not died from cancer in 1990, she would have struggled through the hyperinflation and uncertainty of the years that followed. But by the next decade, she would along with most Russians have got to enjoy relative prosperity. Oil prices rose from around $10 per barrel to a peak of $150 per barrel during the 2000s, filling up the state coffers as Russia sat on one of the world's richest energy reserves. The standard of living rose to unprecedented levels for people of my aunt's generation, with real wages increasing by 10 to 20 per cent each year between 2001 and 2009. The first IKEA opened in Russia in 2000; by 2018, there were eighteen of them, including one in Yekaterinburg. Russia's GDP growth and relative affluence became synonymous with Putin's presidency, which began in 2000. In 1989, my aunt wrote about economic security as a means to an end: she wanted to read, feed the soul and grow as a person. But by 2023, stability and comfort had become an end in itself for most Russians, who had willingly waived their civil liberties in exchange.

Yekaterinburg has changed a lot in the last few years. Because of the pandemic, I had not been to the city since the summer of 2019. As I hadn't visited it on previous trips, I find the city almost unrecognisable. New high-rise residential buildings have mushroomed everywhere; in the 1990s, construction projects paid little attention to complementary aspects of urban design, but now there are new parks and children's playgrounds. Thriving Russian conglomerates have built stunning new offices, such as the headquarters of the Russian Copper Company, designed by the British architects Foster + Partners, of Gherkin fame, and opened in 2021. Old buildings, such as the historic public baths I used to frequent with my grandmother, have been restored and freshly painted. The banks of the Iset River in the centre of Yekaterinburg have been cleaned up and paved. Mothers promenading with buggies point out ducks paddling on the river to their children. Green Grove, a park I remember from school cross-country skiing lessons in winter, used to be popular with drunks and drug addicts. Now it's full of joggers and Nordic walkers.

I get on a trolleybus to visit the yard of the multi-storey building where I lived until the age of sixteen. The Soviet buildings that surrounded my childhood now look brutally unhospitable to me, but in the yard itself I find new flower beds, repainted children's swings and a space rocket I remember climbing myself. Everywhere I walk, I see well-tended neighbourhoods and clean streets. I haven't encountered a single beggar. The 'Z' signs – the unofficial symbol of support for the invasion of Ukraine – have largely disappeared. I've seen the Z only on a few trams and trolleybuses, and on one particularly grotesque banner on the wall of the Ural State Economic University in the city centre.

The city is bursting with new shops, cafes and restaurants. There are obligatory coffee shops with young patrons intently looking at their laptop screens, American-style burger chains, Central Asian eateries offering *plov* and shawarma, upmarket Georgian and Italian restaurants, Burger King and former McDonald's outlets, now rebranded as 'Tasty, Full Stop!' Competing telecom companies advertise brand new iPhones alongside less expensive Chinese smartphone brands. Russian companies bypass economic sanctions via a web of shell companies set up in the West and savvy associates among the neighbouring states. Since spring 2022, Western exports to Kazakhstan, Kyrgyzstan, Armenia and Turkey have surged. Most of these goods are sent on to Russia. Armenia exported $800,000 worth of vehicles to Russia in January 2022; a year later this increased to $180 *million*. Kazakhstan imported €1 million worth of washing machines from the EU in December 2022, four times the amount it did in the December before Russia's invasion of Ukraine. Turkey posted a 97 per cent increase in its exports to Russia between May and July 2022, compared with the same period in 2017–2019. End consumers in Russia now pay more for the same basket of goods, but there is little they can't get hold of – sanctions or not.

I wanted to see if there was prosperity where it mattered most: on the shelves of a regular supermarket. After the withdrawal of many Western brands from the Russian market, local entrepreneurs and established businesses have won space to spread out dozens of their own dairy, confectionery, meat and deli products. Even a small neighbourhood supermarket now displays an enticing variety of cured fish, sausages, artisanal cheeses, bread and pastries. Nestlé, Ferrero, Heinz, Mars and many other Western food corporations are still here too. Since they comply with the Western sanctions on Russia, announcing a stop to advertising campaigns and suspending further investment into the country, it is strange to see so many of their products still available. Perhaps the most interesting section of the supermarket is the shelf with two dozen vodka brands. I expected to see pseudo-patriotic labels, but instead I find 'Little White Birch Tree', 'Five Lakes', 'Snow Peaks', 'Little Winter Village', 'Baikal', 'Tundra', 'Archangelsk' and 'Quail'.

It seemed the propagandists realised they had overdone it

initially with the war rhetoric and the letter 'Z'. With no victories to shout about, the Kremlin softened its oratory, and everyone else followed suit. The messaging has shifted from guns to butter.

At the theatre, too, I find nothing but light entertainment. Yekaterinburg theatres advertise *Cinderella, Amadeus, Bride for Hire, Hunting for Men* and *Henpecked*. The only tragedy permitted is *Romeo and Juliet*. The absence of anything more critical felt strange only once I was back in London. In Yekaterinburg, theatre posters fit seamlessly into the impeccably peaceful city ambience.

Even people who had worked for independent media and lost their jobs because of the Kremlin crackdown have since found their footing in less controversial pastures. Maxim Putintsev worked as a radio journalist for over twenty years. He was the local franchise editor of the independent radio station Echo of Moscow, which frequently interviewed opposition politicians, academics and media personalities on air. On 1 March 2022 the station was abruptly taken off air. It didn't lose its licence and was not accused of any wrongdoing (the charge of 'dissemination of false information and extremism' came later). Echo of Moscow was simply switched off, and a few days later its frequency was filled by Radio Sputnik under the patronage of Margarita Simonyan, head of the Kremlin TV channel, Russia Today. The owner of the Echo of Moscow franchise in Yekaterinburg had other radio stations in his portfolio, which fortunately meant that most people kept their jobs, now curating pop music and local cultural events instead. Putintsev took on a role as head of PR and publicity at the Yekaterinburg football club, Ural, owned by the government of the Sverdlovsk region and backed by a local conglomerate.

Of course, it is not at all uncommon for a journalist to turn to PR. But it is indicative of a remarkable reversal of prestige in the 2020s Russia. Following decades of Soviet stagnation, generations of Russians born in the 1960s and later strove to run their own businesses. Previously, trade was looked down on as a profession, but in the 1990s, becoming a *kommersant* (a man of commerce) was the new aspiration. The bookstores were flooded with Western guides on leadership and start-up know-how. Many Russians became entrepreneurs or joined small- and medium-sized companies. But now, speaking to my family and friends, I see a different trend. Most aspire to work for the government or a prosperous conglomerate, inevitably linked to the Kremlin. As many formerly privately owned Western assets have been reassigned to Russian companies, it is also the sector that is currently recruiting. Besides, a job in IT or any role for a government ministry makes one immune from conscription. The basic instinct of self-preservation trumps any other ambition.

A friend of mine arrives for coffee in a Land Rover he bought a year ago, and I offer him this argument. He tells me that Putin's trump card is comfort. 'Life is good. There is work and plenty of money. If you want to go on holiday to Europe, go ahead – no one is stopping you. If you want to start your own business, there is grant money for that. As you can see, the city is thriving.' When I try to ask him about the war and the cost of this visible comfort, he shrugs and pulls up his iPhone to check his emails. This line of enquiry is the social equivalent of 'Have you filed your tax return?' Having barely spent any time with me, he pays for my coffee and leaves, heading to an award ceremony celebrating local businesses. I stick around to make some notes.

Three men sit at a table next to me. A ten-year-old boy is eating cake. His grandfather is sipping tea while the boy's father is agitated about the situation in Gaza. 'The Israelis are vicious,' he laments. 'They are killing civilians – what animals!' I hesitate, then zip up my coat and leave.

Outside it is dark. I wander down the street pondering Orwell's clairvoyant 'doublethink'. The well-known concept is originally described in *Nineteen Eighty-Four* as the ability to hold mutually contradictory opinions: to forget what is necessary to forget and to tell lies without being aware of doing so. It seems to describe today's Russia eerily well. There is nothing here to suggest that the war is being fought in Ukraine. Ignorance provides people with, if not strength, then certainly comfort. The man I over-heard in the cafe would probably say that the war in Ukraine is about 'peace' while condemning the conflict between Israel and Palestine as 'war'. After two decades of state TV propaganda, I would not be surprised if he had reached that conclusion of his own accord. Generations after the first Soviet habits of double-think were formed, the more prosperous Russians of the 2020s can see and unsee, gloat and mourn, know and unknow.

Khmeli Suneli is a large, popular restaurant in the centre of Yekaterinburg serving Georgian food. In the winter months, the warm interior, with carpets, soft furnishings and a large open kitchen with clay ovens where they bake bread is particularly enticing, and I find the restaurant full even on a weeknight. As I make my way to my table, Russian waiters dressed in sombre tunics are serving plates of steaming *khinkali* dumplings, bar-becued meat and irresistible *khachapuri* – a kind of cheese-filled bread. Russians have always loved Georgian cuisine, and this hasn't changed, despite Russia currently occupying about 20 per cent of the country, a fact not many Russians realise.

I must be careful now. I'm here to meet a group of friends

I worked with briefly in the late 1990s before I left to study in Britain. We haven't been closely in touch, but when I said I'd be in Yekaterinburg they happily agreed to meet me for dinner. I don't know their politics, but I wouldn't want to probe it in a public place. I resolve to sit, listen and enjoy the food I don't get the chance to eat often. We order a bottle of Tsinandali and, as is custom, Marina raises a glass. 'For peaceful skies!' I hear this novel toast often during the course of my stay in Russia.

'We don't talk about politics,' Marina elaborates later. 'That topic is banned in my family and from all of my WhatsApp groups. People are tired of this thing.'

I quickly catch on to what 'this thing' is, but I cannot resist. 'But you do talk about it at home with your husband and son?'

'My youngest is too little,' she says, referring to a twelve-year-old. 'As for my husband, I want to protect my marriage.'

'Oh Jana, don't you start!' says Lena, and I dutifully concentrate on the menu.

Waiting for our starters, we reminisce about old times. They are all some years older than me and started their careers at the Yekaterinburg offices of foreign companies like Lufthansa, Toyota, Indesit and Pfizer. They got jobs in sales, marketing and finance at a time when opportunities were plentiful. Everything was new and exciting: buying media time, opening a car showroom and marketing new drugs like Viagra. The worst thing that happened was Russia's default in August 1998. It was a crazy period of uncertainty with skyrocketing prices, but, in hindsight, the economy actually picked up quickly, thanks to rising oil prices, and the period of painful adjustment to the more realistic dollar exchange rate was brief. Being good at what they do, my friends built successful careers, bought their first cars in their twenties, got married and raised children. These days they all work for Russian companies. The foreign expats we used to have as our bosses and mentors are a distant memory.

It just so happens that Marina, Lena and Yulya's children now study abroad. They are all proud parents whose sons and daughters got into top universities in China, Germany and the Czech Republic to study demanding subjects: biochemistry, engineering and IT after first having mastered Mandarin, German and Czech. The conversation centres around complicated travel arrangements. The Hungarian consulate in Yekaterinburg, where you can get a visa for Europe, is still open. There aren't direct flights to Prague or Frankfurt, so the mothers are having to work out the best routes, via Istanbul or Baku, to visit their children and for their children to come home in the summer. It's not cheap either. In a way, it's a similar conversation I hear in London when someone is complaining about a longer flight time to Tokyo or Seoul, but there is a difference I needn't spell out.

The mothers are worried about Russophobia in Europe. They heard Russian students were being harassed in the Czech Republic, and Lena knew of a friend of a friend who was fired from a German carmaker for being Russian. I point out that a German carmaker's HR department would know better than to commit such a blunder, and I ask why is it always 'a friend of a friend' who gets discriminated against for being Russian?

I quickly correct myself and compliment the delightful aubergine rolls with garlic and walnuts. Our *khinkali* arrive next: they are large dumplings filled with minced lamb, veal, beef and pork. The steamed meat inside is hot and juicy. They are delicious.

I say, 'I don't eat meat all that often – this is a real treat!'

'Why is that? I hear from my daughter that even chicken is crazy expensive in Germany.'

'Yes, organic meat and poultry can be very expensive, but it's

not otherwise. It's more about the climate.' As I say that, I realise that I don't have the right vocabulary to discuss the climate
crisis in Russian. It's not something at the top of the agenda here,
unlike in London. But surely the environment is something we
can actually agree on? I explore the subject but discover that,
despite frequent forest fires around Yekaterinburg, global warm-
ing and even the simplest initiatives to mitigate it do not seem
relevant here. When I ask if they do any recycling at home, Lena
replies that if the government told her to recycle, she would.

'Climate crisis or not,' says Marina, 'I hear gas, electricity and
even water are so expensive in Europe that people can't afford
to use the toilet indoors. A friend of my cousin was visiting his
former classmate in Germany and was told to go outside.'

I roll my eyes. Not a friend of a friend again . . .

I want to say something about Russia's decision to suspend
the supply of gas to some of its European buyers in 2022, which
resulted in the energy price hike in Europe, but I think better
of it. Here, inside the restaurant, it is hot enough for me to be
uncomfortable in my sweater, and I wish I was wearing a T-shirt
instead. I would later find that every cafe and apartment here are
heated to the max. Instead of the jumpers and thermal layers I
am used to wearing in winter in London, I should have packed
light shirts.

'We live well, life is good. Maybe some people are affected by
forest fires, or they struggle to get adequate healthcare using free
services, but I can only judge by my own standard of living. My
family is happy, and it's all that matters,' says Yulya.

'You know,' echoes Marina, 'the problem with people who
don't support the government is that they cannot quite accept
that they are in the minority. The majority of Russians are genuinely happy with Putin.'

'So why shut down opposition?' I ask. 'Let Alexei Navalny criticise government corruption.'

'Corruption has always been prevalent in Russia. It is what it is.'

'But some people might think differently. Aren't they entitled to voice their opinion? It's called democracy.'

'Russia isn't suited for democratic rule. We are better off with a tsar.'

'Even if the tsar locks up activists like Kara-Murza for saying "No to war!"?'

'Don't be naive,' says Yulya. 'An ordinary person has never even heard of him. Besides, he broke the law. It's defamation of the Russian Armed Forces. He got what he deserved. Anyone else care about him?'

The others shake their heads.

'Since you brought up the war,' I ask quietly, 'what if they draft your husband?'

'It would be my husband's duty to defend Russia. I would worry about him, of course, but I would support him, as is my duty.'

I am staggered. The others are silent too. The spell is broken by a waiter, who clears the plates and asks if we want dessert.

I shake my head and ask for the bill. I feel suffocated. The room is hazy with shisha smoke from the tables nearby. Apparently, here you can smoke hookah indoors. I consider checking if we can at least agree on this as a health hazard, but I don't have any energy left.

'I'm sorry,' says Marina. 'We should never have opened up that Pandora's box. This is why we never talk about all that nonsense.'

I look up at Lena.

'I believe that whatever the government decides, they know

best. Thanks to Putin, the economy has recovered after the chaos of the early 1990s. Look around you. Why wouldn't I trust the Kremlin with foreign policy as well?'

I nod. I say I'm exhausted, and they order me a taxi. We hug and wish each other all the best. The car arrives promptly. I thank the driver for not keeping me waiting. He is ethnically Russian and smirks in response. 'It's only *churki* who are always late and incompetent.' I got a dessert after all – a dollop of casual racism. *Churka* is a derogatory Russian word referring to a member of an ethnic minority, especially from Central Asia or the Caucasus. I grit my teeth. Would you have argued with a driver late at night on an icy road?

We pass by the Yekaterinburg opera house, which reminds me of a theatre review I read back in 2021. It seems a lifetime ago. *Mozart. Don Giovanni. Dress Rehearsal* was a new play by the Moscow theatre company Pyotr Fomenko Workshop. In it, a tyrannical theatre director, feared and revered in equal measure, is expected to attend a dress rehearsal of the opera. The company is trembling with anticipation, ready to follow his every whim. Upon hearing the first aria, the director asks for a rifle. He then shoots the actor playing Don Giovanni and asks for an understudy. The dress rehearsal turns into a massacre. What made the production especially compelling was that the audience sat right behind the director's chair. They gasped as the blood spluttered all over the snow-white stage, but they stayed put. After all, it wasn't them being executed on stage. Besides, they had paid good money to see the show.

Chapter 3

Life Goes On

'Where shall we meet?'
   'Outdoors!'
After a day in the city, it's exactly what I need. My friends, Misha and Vera, like hiking as much as I do. They leave the city nearly every weekend to be closer to nature. We head to the Deer Brooks Nature Park, some 120 km south-west of Yekaterinburg in the valley of the River Serga. It was opened about twenty years ago and became a popular destination for school trips and weekend family outings. When it comes to candid conversations, nature trails may even beat the kitchen table.

We drive past weekend roadworks, where lanes are being added to the highway that goes all the way to Moscow. 'This is what ordinary people see: the government is investing in roads,' says Misha. 'War? What war?'

The war, as I saw for myself in Yekaterinburg, isn't visible or audible. The government called its full-scale invasion of Ukraine

a 'Special Military Operation'. A year later, it's been abbreviated
to 'SMO', just one innocuous syllable in Russian. Many people
I spoke to referred to the war as something even more abstract:
'that thing', 'that nonsense', 'that mess' or 'hogwash'.

I have always discussed Russian politics with Vera and Misha,
and I knew they wouldn't mince their words. We haven't seen
each other in person for a while, so I ask them to go back to the
beginning.

'We don't have a TV at home, but I listened to Putin's speech
on the radio on the way to the hospital.' Misha, who is an oph-
thalmologist, had a number of surgeries scheduled that day. 'I
spent the day with the patients, and I had a junior doctor shad-
owing me that day. I went through the motions, but my mind
kept replaying those wild words.'

President Putin addressed the nation on the morning of 24
February 2022 with a long speech accusing the West of 'supporting the far-right nationalists and neo-Nazis in Ukraine', the
people apparently responsible for eight years of 'atrocities' and
'genocide' in the Donbas. He condemned NATO's eastward
expansion, which represented 'an ever mounting and a totally
unacceptable threat to Russia'. Putin gave examples of the
bloody break-up of Yugoslavia and the wars and humanitarian
catastrophes in Iraq, Libya and Syria as a warning that if it did
not act, a similar fate awaited Russia. He also talked about the
West 'seeking to destroy our traditional values and force upon
us their false values, which would erode us from within'. In
response to this 'very real threat to our interests and our very
existence' and citing alleged appeals for help from people of the
Donetsk and Luhansk republics, Putin declared that he had
'made the decision to carry out a Special Military Operation'.
He added, 'We will seek to demilitarise and denazify Ukraine,'

but 'not to occupy Ukrainian territory'. Russia was merely 'defending itself'.

While Misha was in hospital and desperate to read anything other than the official line from the Kremlin as soon as he got home, Vera was in the office rapidly flicking through the various news websites in between her meetings. As a head of department in a large Russian metallurgical company, she had a busy day, interviewing potential new hires, reviewing the latest performance indicators and meeting with her direct reports. She was astounded by the news, but politics wasn't something she'd discussed in the office in the last twenty years. 'At work, we work.' The only unusual thing at the office that day was an internal email from the leadership team addressing all staff and calling for 'togetherness in these difficult times'. At the end of the working day, Vera signed off and rushed home.

She found Misha at the kitchen table glued to the screen. He read out the news he was picking up from local Telegram channels: a man was seen arrested for honking his car horn while driving past a handful of protesters in the city centre; police were seizing people before they had even unrolled their anti-war placards; local activists were collecting food donations to take to detainees. Misha and Vera grabbed tins of condensed milk, packets of biscuits and tea and drove to the collection point. The people they met there were similarly anxious to help and just as helpless. On the way back, their teenage twins called to ask if it was all right to invite some friends over. That night their kitchen was full of youngsters who felt the urgent need to discuss what was happening but couldn't do so in their own homes. Misha and Vera were famous among their twins' classmates for their liberal views, open debates and welcoming kitchen. Misha made cheese toasties. Vera kept topping up everyone's cups of tea.

'We talked about leaving Russia in the first days after the invasion. Within a fortnight that idea lost its legs,' says Misha.

The Bank of Russia imposed a rule forbidding any Russian bank clients to withdraw more than US$10,000 from their dollar and euro accounts. If anyone considered taking out their savings, they had to do so in rubles. Meanwhile, Mastercard and Visa announced they had suspended their operations in Russia. This meant that cards issued in Russia would not work abroad. Russian airlines were no longer welcomed in Europe or the US, and vice versa. Airbnb announced a ban on bookings made from Russia or Belarus. The ruble initially plunged to a record low of 120 to the dollar in March 2022, which stalled spending decisions. Then it recovered to a seven-year high just a few months later, buoyed by the extraordinary international trade and capital-control measures.

'On the one hand, we watched the atrocities in Ukraine, the closing down of independent media, the ban on the BBC and other information resources, arrests of solo protesters who came out with nothing other than a sign saying, "Let's Live in Peace!" and, on the other, we were placed under sanctions, and we felt we weren't welcomed in Europe,' says Misha. 'We felt paralysed. They must have been preparing for it for a long time. The only thing that kept us going at the beginning was that virtually every night our kitchen was packed. Our own friends and our children's friends were desperate to come over and talk things through.'

'In time we came to an inevitable decision,' says Vera. 'Our lives are here: we have our flat, our jobs and our children's school. Misha's parents are here too. He is their only child.'

We have arrived at the gates of Deer Brooks. It's an overcast but dry day at the very end of Pushkin's favourite season, autumn, 'an enchantment for the eyes'. The trees are still dressed in crimson and gold, but the colours are fading. There are a handful of other visitors and school groups, but we have a path to ourselves. I ask Misha about his parents.

'My parents have worked all their lives, they lived through perestroika and have supported me in my career and other choices. They are wonderful grandparents. I see them often but not as often as they see the TV. I'm a patient man, I rarely lose my temper, but things have changed since Crimea. I've had heated arguments with my father, and I suppose we agreed to disagree. The full-scale invasion was a shock. I thought it would be the turning point.'

He falls silent, then continues, kicking away a fallen branch.

'I remember visiting my parents that first weekend. Before I could even say anything, they got worked up about the "Nazis in Ukraine" and I simply lost it. I couldn't get past the official narrative. I left shortly after I'd arrived and didn't call them for a while. It took time, but I think I got to some kind of understanding.' He looks ahead towards the opening in the forest with a view over the River Serga. Larches with their bright yellow needles stand out against the green pines under the bleak sky. 'My parents are from the post-war generation. They were brought up on stories of the horrors of the war, of the great sacrifice and the unity of Soviet people against the enemy. They and their parents built new cities and towns, naming new streets after famous Soviet marshals, after the Great Victory and Peace. They cannot imagine that their country has invaded another. They can't get their heads around the possibility that Russian soldiers kill Ukrainians, our brothers. During the Great Patriotic War we fought together to defeat the German fascists. These images of destroyed residential buildings, people fleeing their homes and hiding underground, rape and plunder – it's inconceivable. So when the state TV shows the army fighting to stand up for marginalised Russian speakers in Eastern Ukraine and portrays the Kyiv government as evil, it's a much more palatable story. It's what they want to believe. When their own son paints a different picture, they get defensive. Aggressively so. They do not want to know.'

We continue in silence. I've heard so many stories like Misha's where people in their forties have fallen out with their parents. Some families stopped talking to each other altogether; others agreed not to talk about politics, as if it were some abstract notion, dissociated from life itself. 'And so,' I finally ask, 'have you given up?'

We are standing on the high bank of the river, taking in the scenery. It's soothing. I half expect Misha to say that family is more important than the truth, but he surprises me.

'No, I don't give up, I can't. My father pushes back, saying he doesn't want to talk about it, but I keep trying. I start with the things I hope we can agree on. He was recently taken to the hospital, where they had no bandages. They asked him to bring his own. My father granted that our healthcare was in a shabby state. Then we agreed that the state should be taking care of the elderly. I tell him about the state of school education, where even hard-working, gifted children need tutors to pass exams to get into universities. Our education system used to be so much better in the Soviet days. I say, "Putin has been in power for the last twenty years, so how come he hasn't addressed all those things?" And finally I ask about the money – what is the state spending its finances on instead?'

Misha explains that small conversations like these establish commonalities and open up some gaps in the official rhetoric that even his parents can see. Unfortunately, the zombification, as some call it, continues day in and day out, as older people tend to watch TV, and all the available channels now propagate the same story. 'So then my father tells me that while Russia is under threat, we first need to defeat the enemy and then we can focus on education and healthcare.' Misha sighs – I suppose in exactly the same way as he does when talking to his parents.

We follow the path along the river and find a table where we can have our picnic: hot soup with rye bread and tea. I ask Misha and Vera to tell me about September 2022, when Putin announced partial mobilisation, drafting reservists who had previously served in the military or had at least completed compulsory military service.

The official announcement was followed by frantic messages via Telegram channels, the new go-to media platform for those who sought alternative information from independent journalists, bloggers and exiled media platforms such as *Novaya Gazeta*. The channels reported that some reservists were handed drafting papers at home or at their place of work. Shirking or desertion meant going to prison, from where there was a high chance you'd be sent to the war front all the same. Mobilisation centres opened in municipal buildings, and even in the foyers of theatres. Someone took a picture of a poster announcing Gogol's *Dead Souls* hanging behind a drafting commission table.

The Ministry of Defence said it was recruiting some 300,000 reservists, but few Russians believed the official numbers. Misha was well aware of the horrific discrepancy between the official deaths from Covid-19 in Russia and the excess deaths during the pandemic, which suggested that as many as a million Russians had died from the coronavirus. Misha wasn't a reservist, but, as a doctor, he was worried that he might be

drafted anyway. He stuck to his routine, but some of his friends
took extra precautions to avoid receiving a physical summons to
serve. One started working from home full-time. He no longer
walked the dog in the morning, delegating the task to his wife
instead. (In 2024, the Russian government began sending
summons for military service electronically.) Another packed
his bag and drove to Kazakhstan, where a line of cars waiting
to cross the border had already formed. He stayed with distant
relatives in Almaty for two months. In total, some 400,000 men
reportedly left Russia after the mobilisation announcement in
September 2022.

'Was anyone drafted from your company?' I ask Vera.

'No one I know,' she replies. 'As far as I understand, big,
strategically important companies like ours are protected by the
Kremlin. They agree to send a few people from the office security and maintenance departments – everyone else is excepted.
The state doesn't call on IT specialists, scientists or engineers. It
tends to recruit people from small towns, rather than cities like
Yekaterinburg.'

'What about those who sign up as mercenaries?'

'These are people who are unemployed or have menial jobs
that don't pay well. Wagner and other private military groups
offer ten times the salary men make as drivers, security guards
or warehouse workers. For them, going to Ukraine is a real opportunity to make money.'

'There was a guy in our children's school who wasn't very academic and left school at the age of sixteen,' says Misha. 'He was a
bit of a loafer, I gather. Then they heard he signed up to join the
army. That was just months before the invasion. First, he served
in the Far East of Russia, then his unit was sent to Ukraine. He
returned home with a bullet in his neck. The doctors can't get it

out; he is disabled for life. But after a few months in the army, he raves to get back to Ukraine. To fight the "Nazis".'

Russia's Ministry of Defence has not been reporting on Russian casualties, which is not surprising. Years after the Afghan and Chechen wars ended, veterans and relatives are still struggling to get accurate public records of the dead. An independent Russian news organisation, Mediazona, and the BBC have verified 74,014 casualties suffered by Russian forces as of October 2024, acknowledging that the total unverified toll is likely to be closer to 200,000, including volunteers from the Donetsk and Luhansk regions. Together with the heavily wounded, Russian losses are likely to be 400,000–560,000.

Back in September 2022 when the Defence Minister Sergei Shoigu announced partial mobilisation of 300,000 reservists, he said that around twenty-five million people in Russia met the enlisting criteria. It was supposed to suggest unlimited reserves.

'You don't think they'll come after you then?' I ask Misha after a while. He shakes his head. 'I don't think so.'

On the way back to the car park, we pass by a few guided groups. The hikers aren't clad in Patagonia, Jack Wolfskin or North Face, instead wearing Chinese and Russian brands I don't recognise, but they look just like any outdoor enthusiasts in the West. Misha and Vera used to travel abroad a couple of times a year. They've been to Austria, Italy, Spain, Turkey and France; they especially love Norway, where they've been on multiple kayaking and hiking trips. Despite the war and partial mobilisation, Russians can still travel abroad. It is, however, complicated. There are fewer available flights to and from Russia, it is much more difficult and expensive to arrange visas and buy foreign currency and there is a degree of uncertainty. There are rumours that the

Kremlin will introduce exit visas or close the borders altogether. Many who like active holidays are now staying in Russia, where thanks to the captive market the tourism industry is growing at a fast pace.

Misha and Vera tell me about their recent trips to St. Petersburg, Murmansk, Karelia in the northwest of Russia and to the Vishera Nature Reserve in the Perm region in the Northern Urals, which is practically 'on our doorstep', a mere ten-hour car journey from Yekaterinburg. There they enjoyed a week of sightseeing, hiking and kayaking on the Vishera River. It is a remote and sparsely populated area with a still-developing tourism industry, but as a reward, you get to enjoy vast mountain vistas, virgin forest hiking trails and the tranquillity of the taiga all to yourself. Further north, in the Komi Republic, they went to see the Manpupuner stone pillars, 30–40-metre-high natural rock formations, which were considered sacred by the local Mansi people. One of the 'Seven Natural Wonders of Russia', it is accessible only by hiking or helicopter. They show me photos – I'm blown away. I've never seen anything like it, and I'm mentally putting Manpupuner on my list of places to visit one day. But holidaying in Russia is an uncomfortable idea for me just now, I tell them.

'I understand,' says Vera. 'Let me tell you about Crimea.'

Vera hadn't ever been to Crimea, and after the annexation she didn't feel right about going on holiday to a Russian-occupied territory. But the Crimean Peninsula is famous for its hiking trails, so Misha persuaded her to go there for a long weekend. It was immediately obvious that a lot of money had been invested there: modern roads and highways, new tourist infrastructure, freshly repainted buildings in the town centres. Carefully, they talked to the locals, who said they were very happy about all the money invested and the increase in tourism.

'One guide we hired told us bluntly that he was happy Russia had taken over. I'm pretty sure he isn't the only one,' says Misha.

'I loved it there,' adds Vera. 'I've permitted myself to go there again. I had nothing to do with what happened with Crimea.'

'Besides,' adds Misha, 'if my taxes are being spent there, I want to see the result.'

Back in the car, I ask my friends about collective responsibility, something we have been discussing in liberal circles since the end of February 2022. Are we, as individuals, accountable for the war? Could we have done more to counter the government propaganda over the years? What are the moral implications of the Kremlin's actions for ordinary Russian people?

'The war doesn't have anything to do with me,' says Vera. 'I will not accept responsibility for what is being done to Ukraine.'

'Am I guilty of the horrific atrocities in Bucha or Mariupol? No,' says Misha. 'The Russian state is responsible for that. The war goes on, but at least some work is already being done, at least in the east of Ukraine, to repair some of the destruction caused. As Russian taxpayers, we are contributing to that.'

I had received the same answers from other like-minded people in Yekaterinburg: 'Being Russian doesn't mean we are to blame for the war.'

I ask if Misha and Vera see any parallels with Hitler's Germany in the 1940s.

'No, I don't,' repeats Vera. 'I don't associate myself with Russia, the aggressor. I refuse to accept any collective responsibility, I'm not part of it.'

Misha says that at the beginning of the full-scale invasion he was thinking about penance and what he would do. 'I wanted to go and help rebuild Ukraine. Now I must confess that I don't see this war ending in our lifetime. Even if some peace agreement is reached, it won't be the end of it. We would need a change of government in Russia to consider the consequences of the military aggression as a nation and to encourage repentance.'

'And we won't see that either,' agrees Vera. 'After Putin, the regime will stay the same. I don't see any other possibility.'

They explain that this is why they are now focusing on their family and, as they call it, their 'little inner world'. They have chosen to stay in Russia, and in doing that they have accepted certain limitations on their freedom. They now talk freely only in private. At work, they work. On social media, they post about their travels, mushroom picking and making raspberry jam. They never criticise the government. Misha would not even bring up the lack of bandages in his father's local hospital in public. They follow these basic rules of self-preservation just like their forefathers did in Soviet times. Fortunately, they have like-minded friends with whom they can gather in their kitchen to discuss political realities. 'Otherwise, the cognitive dissonance would be unbearable,' says Misha.

'We have chosen inner emigration,' says Vera. 'Like Soviet dissidents who lived in the USSR, we do not agree with the state ideology. But since we have stayed in Russia, we cannot confront it. All we can do is look after ourselves and find ways to escape the reality. Nature helps. So do hobbies and personal projects.'

'Let us show you what we mean,' smiles Misha as he turns towards the village of Staroutkinsk.

Some 100 km from Yekaterinburg, Staroutkinsk reminds me of a setting for a Chekhov play. Here, rivulets Utka and Dar'ya fall into the Chusovaya River. The first settlers built their houses on both of its banks. They were Old Believers – Christians who maintained ancient liturgical practices despite the reforms of the

Russian Orthodox Church, introduced by the Moscow patriarch, Nikon, and tsar Alexei in 1652–1666. The most significant of the ritual and textual changes were the spelling of Jesus and the practice of making the sign of the cross with three fingers rather than two. The reforms were aimed at unifying the Russian and Greek Orthodox churches, but not everyone conformed. Old Believers were persecuted, and many fled western Russia to start a new life in the less populated east. They were hard-working peasants who developed agriculture and found peace here in maintaining their faith. Later, in the eighteenth century, the Demidovs, early Russian industrialists, were granted a licence to develop iron ore in the northern Urals. The Demidovs needed reliable labourers, and they found them in the Old Believers, who were deeply religious (i.e., they didn't drink) and hard-working. The Demidovs built one of their plants along the Chusovaya River. The plant in Staroutkinsk processed metal ore and produced cast and binding metal. The industry remained viable until the 1990s. After production had been shut down, the village's population halved to about 3,000. Now, thanks to the enviable setting by the River Chusovaya, new dachas are being built here for people who live and work in Yekaterinburg.

Misha opens the gate and ushers me into their house. Nestled on a high riverbank, it is a one-storey building, flanked by a pine grove. Inside, it is still a work in progress. We traverse wooden planks towards the open living space with Misha taking the role of tour guide. I pause by the window to take in the magnificent view. Below the terrace unfolds a generous garden, thoughtfully landscaped with apple and pear trees, flower beds and vegetable patches – an homage to the classic Soviet dacha. Beyond the fence, a path leads to the river, which meanders through evergreen forest and fields. Misha and Vera began looking for a plot during the pandemic. With the help of an architect, they meticulously designed the house, planning to retire one day from the bustling metropolis. Over the past two years, they have devoted themselves to overseeing the construction, watching their dream project come to life.

Outside, Misha makes a fire. He is grilling meat and foil-wrapped potatoes over coals. Vera slices bread and opens a can of homemade marrow caviar. We sip tea with mint, sage and thyme she grew in her garden. With dinner, Misha pours us potent raspberry liquor. It's sweet and smells of a now distant summer. I propose a toast to the dacha. We drink.

'*This* is our future,' says Misha. 'In a country with no opposition, no free elections, no other opinion, no prospect of social liberalisation, we have to carve out a little world for ourselves.'

'In the summer, we will have a guest room for you. We can go kayaking or paddleboarding. In August, we will pick mushrooms by the bucketload. Come and stay with us,' says Vera.

'It is the dream,' I agree.

We sit by the fire for what seems like hours. We talk about the Russian opposition organisations abroad who don't seem to be able to agree on anything, which only plays into Putin's hands. We sigh over the jailed activists and journalists in Russia. Any protest or dissent is impossible now. Vera and Misha worry about the twins and their future. We talk about Staroutkinsk and people they've met here. 'Our people,' says Misha, referring to the liberal-minded couples in their forties who have built dachas here. The conversation weaves its way to the question preoccupying me the most. What prompted Misha and Vera to think critically of the government in the first place when other Russians sided with the Kremlin? I remind Vera of our former classmates at our prestigious state school, who later, like her,

went to the top universities in Yekaterinburg, built careers, got
married, had children. They've holidayed in Europe and Asia
many times. They can access any information on the internet
via a VPN. Smart and successful, they still support Putin – and
I want to try to understand their point of view. I wait for Vera to
speak. She's been staring at the flames for a long time.

'Have I ever told you about my grandmother?' she finally
asks. 'My grandparents were both Jewish. Lenin famously spoke
against the pogroms, but under Stalin, the government rein-
troduced internal passports with a line for ethnicity. Having
the word 'Jew' in a Soviet passport wasn't going to get you any
favours. During the Stalinist purges, thousands of Jews were
tried, exiled and murdered on various pretexts. In January 1938,
my grandfather, who was a senior consultant at the Ministry of
Agriculture in Moscow, was arrested for "taking part in counter-
revolutionary terrorist activities". My grandmother found the
prison where he was being kept and brought him the home-
cooked food she was allowed to pass on. Later, he was transferred
to another prison, and she continued to bring him tea, sugar –
whatever she could get – for years. She always took my mother,
who was just a toddler. They never got to see him. After Hitler
invaded in June 1941, Stalin decreed that all 'unreliables' be sent
away from Moscow. Grandmother moved to Ryazan, some 200
km south-east from the capital. She didn't stay long; her landlady
told her that when the Germans got there, she would denounce
her as a Jew. Frightened for her daughter's future, Grandmother
left for Sverdlovsk, as Yekaterinburg was called back then. Her
brother, recently evacuated to the Urals from Kharkov, took her
in. She found a job in some canteen. They survived.'

Vera pauses. Her late mother was a woman of few words but
a brilliant scientist who was denied a place in the Soviet space

programme in late 1950s, presumably because of that ethnicity line in her passport.

'In September 1956, under Khruschev, my grandfather's reputation was rehabilitated. My grandmother was told that he had died in prison from heart failure. Only, in the late 1980s, during the period of glasnost, our family found out that my grandfather had been shot in April 1938, just three months after his arrest. It was the prison guards whom his wife had been feeding all that time in Moscow.

'My grandmother lived with us. She had her own little room but spent most of her time in the kitchen. It was she who taught me how to make marrow caviar and how to brew tea with herbs. She was perfectly lucid well into her eighties. I spent a lot of time with her after school, as both of my parents worked late. When I was old enough, Grandmother told me about Stalin and what he had done to her husband and her. I remember it vividly: she shook with anger. I will never forget that.' Vera paused, looking at the embers. 'Or take what the government tells me at face value.'

On the way back to Yekaterinburg we stop at a petrol station to get a coffee for Misha, who is driving. It's dark and cold outside. The brightly lit station has eager uniformed attendants, a cafe with a purring coffee machine and an extensive variety of sweet and savoury snacks. Misha orders a latte and insists on buying me a hot chocolate. It is very good. Back in the car, Vera tells me about an art museum I should try to visit while I'm in town. Misha asks me about the hiking trips I have planned for later in the year. Life goes on.

Chapter 4

Churchill's Key

Many recall Churchill's famous remark on Russia, 'It is a riddle wrapped in mystery inside an enigma', but few remember what he said in full. Responding to Russia signing a non-aggression pact with Hitler in 1939, Churchill also said that 'perhaps there is a key. That key is Russian national interest.'

In Russia, it's elementary. You only need to open a school textbook.

I managed to get my hands on the latest edition of a Russian history textbook, aimed at seventeen- to eighteen-year-olds in their final school year. I studied the equivalent textbooks from 1995–1996, when turbulent current affairs had demolished the foundations of Russia's twentieth-century history. It is hard to imagine what it must have been like for our history teachers to discuss the Bolshevik Revolution, the 1920s Civil War or the Soviet regime under Stalin. It was during the 1990s that the government opened the previously closed archives exposing the scale of Stalinist atrocities in full. The textbooks in my final school year could not possibly keep up with the changes happening in Russia at the time, and it was equally futile to expect much from teachers; like all state employees, their salaries were squeezed by head-spinning inflation, and their primary concern wasn't pedagogy, but livelihood. Times have changed. In 2023, teachers' pay is still lower than an average Russian salary (less than US$10,000 a year), but now textbooks are printed on premium colour paper, fully updated – even for the events of 2022 – and presenting a narrative the teachers are presumably encouraged to follow verbatim.

It goes like this: behind calls for democracy and promotion of global trade, the United States and its British allies have always followed their own interests, often disregarding international law. It is they who invaded Iraq, always supported Israel against its Arab neighbours and worked to alienate the rest of Eastern Europe from Russia in order to get their hands on lucrative energy contracts. The goal of the US and its allies is to weaken and then break up Russia, ultimately taking over its natural resources. Their first torpedo triggered the conflict between Russia and Georgia over Abkhazia and South Ossetia in 2008. Then, as Ukraine refused to pay market prices for Russian gas, so the narrative goes, the West fuelled Russophobia in Kyiv and organised a *coup d'état* to install its own puppet government. Russian-speaking citizens of Crimea and Eastern Ukraine refused to recognise it. (It helped that the Russian navy had a base on the Crimean Peninsula and ensured order and security there.) Crimea voted to join Russia, while Donetsk and Luhansk have been fighting for independence from Kyiv since 2014. The US funded Volodymyr Zelenskyy's army and built secret biological labs in Ukraine, preparing for war with Russia. Churchill has an honorary mention in history textbooks as an 'uncompromising politician', but 'today even he would think that the Western world has lost its marbles'. The situation became untenable. In February 2022, Putin resolved to help Donetsk and Luhansk and launched a 'special operation' as a preventative measure to safeguard Russia's security.

This national interest narrative is consistent with the prevalent Kremlin rhetoric. But much like the media, the textbook is peppered with misrepresentations and fabrications. The Russian constitutional reform of 2020 is said to have strengthened civil society and the individual rights of citizens. Referring to the escalation of animosity between the US and Russia, the textbook alleges that at a conference in Vilnius in 2006, then-US Vice President Dick Cheney said that Russia 'will become an enemy' if it doesn't allow its neighbouring states to welcome democracy. In fact, he said, 'None of us believes that Russia is fated to become an enemy,' a subtle but important difference, easily checked via the White House archives online. But it's not the falsehoods that stand out. It's the tone of the narrative. Some ten years ago I started picking up on the aggressive tone my father had adopted when discussing politics with me. It's the same hostility spat out on the evening talk shows on state TV channels. The language too has morphed from the courteous style of the Soviet intelligentsia to the lingo of the criminal underworld. It started in 1999 during the war with Chechnya with Putin's promise to pursue terrorists all the way: 'If we catch them on the toilet, we will wipe them out in the outhouse.' Two decades later, the same vernacular is being used in a children's textbook, where NATO advisers are said to have 'coached' Zelenskyy to wage war on Donbas, deploying the informal word *nataskali*, normally used to describe dog training.

At the end of each section, there are questions for students to ponder. 'What helped Russia recover its leading position in international relations between 2008 and 2022?' If some seventeen-year-old struggles to answer that, other questions are designed to help: 'What kind of weapons does Russia have to ensure its military advantage? Why is it important to have a best-in-class military arsenal? What are the reasons that forced Russia to launch its Special Military Operation? And why have the majority of Russians supported it?'

These questions are not there to encourage critical thinking. The afterword to the textbook has a clear message to the younger generation: 'History educates citizens about their rights and duties.' The latter, in today's Russia, have only one connotation. As for citizens' rights, will they even make it into the next year's edition?

Still, how does defending national interest justify an attack on another country? I pose this question to my cousin. Like me, Dima is an only child. He grew up hanging out with mates in the yards of Soviet apartment blocks, rather than reading books. As a teenager, he mastered martial arts, which became popular in Russia in the late 1980s.

'Do you know the first principle of a street fight?' he asks me. 'Hit first.'

'I don't like the war,' he continues. 'Young men are dying on both sides. But Russian men are sacrificing their lives so that I can enjoy peace and have a good life.'

Dima is a fifty-year-old businessman who has lived in Yekaterinburg all his life. He has been abroad, but only on holidays. In Russia, he has travelled extensively both for work and for leisure. To him, it is strange that I chose to live on a tiny island like Britain when I could have stayed in the vastest country in the world. In Russian, the word *neob'yatnaya* (vast) derives from 'impossible to embrace or conquer'. For Dima, Russia's size is synonymous with opportunity. As a married man and a father of three, he thinks a good life is about having a 'traditional' family, something he wants for me as well. He says, 'God willing, you will meet someone soon and find your happiness.'

Dima is one of many Russians who found God and embraced Orthodox Christianity, despite having grown up without any religion. When we were growing up, the word 'god' still featured in the Russian language, but it was used as mindlessly as one says 'Bless you!' in English. It hadn't even occurred to me that the Russian word *spasibo*, which means 'thank you', comes from 'God save you' until my English boss pointed it out to me when I was in my twenties. As a child, I thought that only uneducated people believed in God, and growing up in the Soviet Union with free primary, secondary and higher education, there weren't many believers around. There were maybe two churches – both locked up and crumbling down – still standing in my hometown before perestroika. If my maternal grandmother prayed, she did so in private. Things changed very rapidly under Gorbachev. God came into fashion so swiftly that my father decided to have himself – and me – baptised in 1989. (My mother admitted she had been secretly baptised in 1952.) Old churches in Yekaterinburg and other prosperous cities in Russia were restored, and new ones were constructed with private money. Such donations went hand in hand with favours sought, while government officials topped up their state salaries with bribes. Within a decade, newly erected cupolas were shining next to dilapidated hospital buildings.

Putin has used the Russian Orthodox Church to cement his power in Russia. With a nod to the great philosophical debate of 1830s–50s Russia, fought for the soul of the nation between Westerners and Slavophiles, Putin has steered the country away from Western ideals of democracy, progressive reforms, bottom-up economic development and secularism. Instead, he has taken the Slavophiles' three core principles of Orthodoxy, Autocracy and Nationalism as a roadmap. Patriarch Kirill of Moscow has been Putin's ally from the beginning of his ascent to power. The Church has played an instrumental role in portraying Russia as a defender of traditional Christian values, as opposed to Western liberalism and moral relativism, while turning a blind eye to corruption, assassinations and armed conflicts. The Church has framed the war with Ukraine as a righteous struggle, positioning Russia as a spiritual and holy nation in opposition to the sinful West. In this narrative, it's a battle of 'good' versus 'evil'. Patriarch Kirill didn't stop at lurid symbolism; he has repeatedly advocated for self-sacrifice, patriotic duty and even 'spiritual mobilisation' – a term coined in September 2022.

As someone who isn't religious, I have a deep respect for faith – but Christianity in Russia is something I feel sceptical about. People like Dima would say they found God in their hearts, but is it possible to avoid political preaching when attending service in Russia? Dima says he supports 'traditional family values'. This term didn't come out of thin air; it's being broadcast by state media and evangelised in church, whereas homosexuality is castigated as 'unnatural' and 'anti-Christian'. I want to ask him to consider being more tolerant, but I myself struggle to do so when it comes to his newly found faith.

I steer the conversation back to Russia and ask whether he supports Putin.

'You are critical about the current government,' he tells me, 'but you forget that it is hard to manage such a huge country with a difficult past. Every Russian ruler has been a bit of a despot and more than a little corrupt. It's how it is.'

Listening to Dima, I'm transported to some nineteenth-century Russian novel with characters who are resigned to their fate.

'I want Russia to prosper,' he continues. 'Russia is rich in resources, it will always be able to trade, and the Russian people are highly entrepreneurial. I believe in Russia's future, and I contribute to it by growing my business. This and my family are all I care about.'

It is a picture I'm getting here again and again: ordinary people choose to focus on things within their control.

'I am Russian and Russia is me,' says Dima.

It's his upbringing, his set of values and his future. We say goodbye and I ponder: if I had stayed in Yekaterinburg, would I too be praising Russia's resources and size, seeing the West as 'other', seeking solace in church and expressing reservations about non-heterosexuality?

I'm looking up at smart high-rises in a new residential neighbourhood that could be in Hamburg, Chicago or Toronto. My childhood friend Katya bought an apartment here recently, as befits a successful executive recently appointed CEO of a growing local enterprise. I head to a wine store next to a swanky-looking gym. Other ground-floor businesses in this prestigious development include a nursery, a yoga studio, a pharmacy, a supermarket and a few eateries. The upmarket wine store has a section of Russian wines, but most of its shelves feature the best of Tuscany, Bordeaux, Rioja and the Douro Valley.

'Oh yes,' says Katya, hugging me and nodding to the concierge of her building, 'you can get whatever you want in Yekaterinburg:

French champagne, an Apple iPhone or a German car. You just have to pay a little more than you used to.'

Katya and I met at primary school and were close, often monopolising our landlines as we compared maths homework after school. If Katya solved a problem I couldn't tackle, it spurred me to find a solution. We drifted apart later, especially after I left Russia, but stayed in touch, mostly on social media. Back in February 2015, I remember posting on Facebook about the assassination of Boris Nemtsov, right in front of the Kremlin. A liberal Russian politician who once served under Boris Yeltsin, Nemtsov was especially vocal about the increasingly authoritarian government and against military intervention in Ukraine. About fifty thousand people joined a peace march in Moscow in March 2014, with Nemtsov leading the way carrying a banner that read 'Hands Off Ukraine'. He spoke at the rally, pronouncing Putin 'a sick man' who had occupied Crimea 'because he wants to rule for ever'. Katya commented on my post saying, 'Who? He is a nobody who ceased to matter in Russian politics a long time ago.' What startled me at the time was not her support for Putin's government, but her swift disregard for one person's life. It was at that time that I began to suspect our values had diverged even further than our political views.

Katya is smart, successful, interested in politics and vocal about her opinions. I'm here to listen and try to understand why she thinks as she does. Inside her apartment there are still some boxes lining the corridor walls. Katya explains that she's been too busy to unpack; some of her best engineers were called to the front, and the job market is currently hot as growing local businesses compete for the best specialists. The property market, too, is booming: this new neighbourhood is already expanding, with Katya's high-rise building set to be completed soon. Most of the flats in it have already been sold. Katya leads me to the kitchen with an adjacent living room. The bar-style table is laden with a selection of half a dozen cheeses, fruit, olives and other delicacies. Katya apologises for not having time to cook but encourages me to try the local cheeses. The dairy industry has really leapt forward in recent years.

'Every cloud has a silver lining,' says Katya. 'I genuinely thought that the Russian economy would be hindered by the sanctions, but the opposite has happened. We are growing, while Western companies have lost a huge market here. European politicians hurt their own business interests.'

'That may be true, but most people in the West think it's a price worth paying. In any case, the sanctions haven't worked, as I've seen for myself, and the war is ongoing.' Since Katya doesn't flinch, I decide not to beat around the bush. 'Tell me, what is Russia doing in Ukraine?'

'Securing its borders.'

'From?'

'The US, Britain, NATO – the West – who want to weaken, then break up Russia and take over its natural resources. As you know, Europe doesn't have much, and the US wants to have full control over the global energy market.'

A week ago, I might have flinched, but after watching TV in Russia, speaking to my father and reading the history textbook, I'm now well versed in this narrative.

'And Ukraine?'

'Ukraine is just an unfortunate pawn. I feel sorry for people there.'

'Putin has shown the world Russia's military capability, hundreds of thousands of people have died – both Ukrainians and Russians. Millions have been displaced. Isn't it enough? What happens next?'

'There will be no Ukraine.'

'What?'

'Vanga predicted it a long time ago.'

Katya explains that Baba Vanga was a blind Bulgarian mystic who died in the 1990s, but not before making a few predictions, including the break-up of the Soviet Union, the Chernobyl disaster and even that the 44th president of the United States would be African American. I would once have sneered at her superstition, but not so long ago Dame Donna Langley, chairman of the NBC Universal Studio Group in the US, talked about consulting tarot cards on *Desert Island Discs*, so having Russian executives refer to mystics and clairvoyants is perhaps not that ludicrous. Horoscopes have remained stubbornly popular in Russia since they first appeared in the 1990s. Perhaps people here find some relief in that the war and other disasters have been predestined.

Over the course of the evening, I reflect on Katya's worldview that Russian people are special. They are strong and resilient, which helps them endure hardship. Russians are smart and entrepreneurial, which is how they survived the drastic transformation from a command economy to a market one. Russians are spiritual.

'All allegations about Bucha etc., are fabricated. A Russian wouldn't loot, rape or kill civilians,' says Katya, who genuinely thinks that Russians are a superior people. Her nationalist views don't surprise me. She has lived in Yekaterinburg all her life, where she graduated from school and university at the top of her class and built a successful career. She reads widely and consumes global media; she's been abroad, but only to admire European capitals or relax at seaside resorts. By contrast, I enrolled in an international school in Germany at sixteen before going on to Oxford. I met so many super-smart people from all over the world during high school and my undergraduate years that I later chose to live in cosmopolitan London precisely because of its high-achieving and diverse culture. Coming to Russia now shocks me because of how white and homogenous life is – how the same pop stars grace TV screens decades later and nearly everything, from food to branding, has a touch of nostalgia. This idea of Russian superiority isn't shocking or new – it was planted here as a Soviet concept a century ago, if not earlier, under the tsars, and no one, not even the opposition, has challenged it since.

Katya's views are educating me in how business leaders in Russia see its future. She sees sanctions and other policies to isolate Russia as a challenge that will only spur it on to develop its own industries. I apologise for being rude, but I point out that while the fresh goat cheese is delicious, 'Russian Camembert' is rubbery if not inedible. Don't most successful economies play to their competitive advantage? 'We'll get there,' says Katya. I recognise that stubbornness in her. She is quick to remind me that Russian IT specialists now work all over the world, and she is convinced that many will return to Russia. 'Who really wants to live in the States, where children shoot each other at school, or in Europe, where capital cities are filled to the brim with migrants from Africa? It will only get worse. Meanwhile, IT specialists here are exempt from military service, they are offered mortgages at special rates and only pay thirteen per cent income tax.'[1] She tells me about her nephew who is already a computer whizz thanks to IT education at school. 'He is the future of this country and will be snapped up by any cyber security firm or the military. *My nash, my novy mir postroim.*'

'We will build our own new world', a line from the Russian

---

1. Russia has since introduced a progressive income tax system, effective from 1 January 2025.

translation of Eugène Pottier's 'The Internationale', adopted by the Bolsheviks as the first Soviet national anthem in 1918, is still in use. I'm tempted to point out that no one has asked people around here for their vision of the future, not for a while, but instead I ask about Russia's ambitions beyond its borders.

'How big is this new world?'

'Russia isn't an imperialist country – it's nonsense. We aren't trying to conquer the world. Our only goal is to defend our national interests. Russia is one of the few countries in the world that has genuine sovereignty,' she continues. 'Ukraine is a puppet; Britain, and even France and Germany, have their policies dictated by Washington. Russia steps in to defend separatists in Ukraine, Transnistria, Abkhazia and South Ossetia. Russia stood up for the Serbs when NATO bombed Yugoslavia. Do you really think the world should be unipolar?'

In that context, Katya is upset that Poland, Estonia, Latvia and Lithuania have sided with the West and are decidedly anti-Russia. 'Poles should be grateful we liberated them from German Nazis. As for the Baltics, they had nothing but tinned fish. We fed and dressed them, sold them energy at discounted rates, but instead of saying thank you, they hate us.'

It would be easy to refute Katya's arguments. The Soviet Union annexed eastern territories from Poland in 1939 following the Molotov–Ribbentrop Pact with Germany. In 1940, the Soviet Union occupied Estonia, Latvia and Lithuania. It is no mystery why those countries are wary of Russia. Similarly, in 1979, Soviet ambitions in Afghanistan certainly went beyond helping fellow communists. The massacre in Bucha in Ukraine in 2022 has been well documented by international agencies. But facts won't change her mind – or the minds of people like her.

The real issue here is emotional. People crave belonging. Putin understood it well from the outset. His historical escapades need not be true as long as they tell a good story. And his narratives are closely reminiscent of Russian *bylinas* – epic tales of noble ancient knights who defend their lands and those who have been wronged. Original *bylinas* told stories of 'how it was', loosely based on historical facts but greatly embellished to spin a good yarn. In the 1930s, *bylinas* as a genre became politicised with the state ordering storytellers to create new Soviet epics featuring heroes of the Civil War: Chapayev, Lenin and, of course, Stalin. Performers were sent far and wide to tell and sing new Soviet tales commemorating important events and contemporary heroes in the same *bylina* style. A song about Stalin's wisdom, likened to magnificent pine trees and mighty rivers, helped legitimise his power through folklore. Today, schoolchildren are encouraged to create *bylinas* about Vladimir Putin. One such tale, published online in 2011 on a portal for gifted children, glorifies Vova (a diminutive of Vladimir) for doing great deeds for Mother Russia: teaching Ukraine a lesson (for not paying for Russian gas), earning respect from the West and righting other wrongs. 'What a knight, Volodyushka [another diminutive], Mother Russia is mighty proud of him!' Other forms of traditional Russian culture, such as live choral singing, are back too and are also used to shower praise upon Vladimir Putin. Thankfully, this genre is limited to official state concerts and TV broadcasts.

Whether it's a *bylina* or a president's speech, at their core these stories pitch a battle between good and evil. The Russian state, of course, takes the righteous side: from the return of Crimea to defending Russian-speaking Ukrainians from neo-Nazis, it's always a case of wronged Russia against the Wicked West. And who wouldn't want to be on the side of 'good'? Katya tells me they have an informal lunchtime club in the office where people can discuss politics. I doubt there is much debate in the current climate, though it sounds like a club you'd join if you wanted to advance your career. But mostly people make up their minds for less bombastic reasons than the Kremlin narrative. Many ordinary people agree that Russian athletes have been wronged by the West: beloved figure skaters or ice hockey players can no longer compete internationally. This 'wrong' is then compounded by another 'wrong', like Russian bank cards no longer being accepted abroad or Airbnb blocking its services to Russia-based users, and suddenly millions of politically ambivalent people side with the Kremlin.

What only a few years ago was a bystander society has morphed into the 'aggressively obedient majority', a term first coined in 1989 by the Russian historian and democrat Yury Afanasyev. Talking to people here in Yekaterinburg, I've heard how people who were first shocked by the invasion came round to support the war. The arguments range from 'How long did Russia have to tolerate what was being done to Russian-speakers in Ukraine? It was high time to smash the fascists,' to 'We might as well finish what we started,' to 'Russia can't lose face – we must win.' I fear that this majority sentiment will harden, like limescale, and stay for generations.

We leave politics for a while. I admire the view of the city through the windows and peck at the food. Katya tells me about her life outside of work: she spends time with her family and friends and goes to Zumba classes. Her guilty pleasure is Turkish soap operas. We reminisce about our childhood, when together with our mothers and grandmothers we would watch Brazilian, US and Australian soaps. *Santa Barbara* and *Return to Eden* were among our favourites. We lapped it all up: people living in their own houses rather than in nearly identical flats, female executives running businesses, beautiful sandy beaches and romance that was much more explicit than in the Soviet movies. We loved Roxette and Whitney Houston, playing the soundtrack to the film *The Bodyguard* on repeat. In the difficult 1990s, we focused on getting good grades at school and dreamt of the new opportunities opening up for us now that Russia was no longer a closed, isolated country. It's hard to believe the West has become the enemy now.

'Russia isn't the aggressor,' says Katya. 'We stood up to the burgeoning nationalism in Ukraine. Otherwise, we have no motive to attack anyone, Europe least of all. Many Russian children study there. Russians own a lot of real estate. But NATO keeps expanding, and we are forced to defend our safety.' Katya is exasperated, I can see.

'Will it be possible for Russia to reconcile with the West?'

'Not in the near future. Sanctions, anti-Russian propaganda and geopolitical manoeuvres that harm our interests have tarnished the relationship between us. It's the "Iron Curtain 2.0". In the meantime, Russia has already reoriented its economy towards Asia, Africa and the Middle East. The BRICS union is growing.'[2]

In Katya's view, Russia is re-balancing the concentration of global power away from the hegemony of the United States. It would be a positive development if only Russia wasn't fearmongering with its nuclear arsenal.

'Russia has always been open to talks,' says Katya. 'We will never use nuclear weapons. But it is a deterrent.'

'We were brought up on the cult of peace after the Great

---

2. BRIC was originally formed in 2006 by Brazil, Russia, India and China. South Africa joined in 2010 (hence, BRICS); Egypt, the UAE, Iran and Ethiopia joined in January 2024; Algeria, Belarus, Bolivia, Cuba, Indonesia, Kazakhstan, Malaysia, Nigeria, Thailand, Turkey, Uganda, Uzbekistan and Vietnam were added as alliance partners in October 2024.

Patriotic War and watched broken men return from Afghanistan, and yet we are passing on the world at war to the next generation. Don't you think it's strange?'

'We grew up with an illusion of peace. Wars are inevitable. As for the next generation, they don't care about wars or national boundaries. They are completely apolitical. They move abroad to work for Google or to start their own tech businesses.'

I make a mental note to seek out Russians in their twenties who now live abroad.

I also wonder how is it that people of the same age who went to the same school and built enviable careers in Yekaterinburg can have such different opinions. I am thinking of Katya and Vera, whom I saw over the weekend. They grew up just five minutes' walk from each other. Like me, they learned English from the age of seven. They both excelled at school and then at university. They listened to the same music at open-air concerts, drinking Baltika beer. They got married in their twenties, had children and were both close to their parents and their older siblings. I probe it with Katya and eventually we get there. Whereas Vera's parents were academics, Katya grew up in a family where her father and uncle were both in the military. Her grandfather, too, like everyone in that generation, fought in the Second World War. Katya listened to their stories all through her childhood and learned to trust their judgement. Now she also talks to her brother-in-law, who is in the special forces. 'People in the military and intelligence know more than we do.' Unlike a typical Westerner, used to having their politicians grilled on every subject by the media and the opposition, a Russian who grew up in the Soviet Union may have internalised the notion that 'the leadership knows best'.

'Don't you want to have freedom of information, the ability

to express and hear opposing views, free and fair elections?'
I ask.

'Ah, it's not important. We have other values.'

I shake my head, then laugh. Katya had told me many times
before that I had been indoctrinated with Western values by
the BBC.

'Do you mean a sense of national unity, which trumps individual freedoms?'

'Yes,' she says, 'but it's not just that. Russians aren't impatient
or impulsive like some people in the West. You know well what
people here endured over the course of the twentieth century.'

I nod, thinking of the Civil War after the Bolshevik
Revolution, the Stalinist purges, the Second World War and
the 1990s. The period of economic reforms set in motion by
Gorbachev, which promised to rebuild the economy (the literal
meaning of 'perestroika'), was continued by Yeltsin, who was
advised to apply 'shock therapy' to the critically ill patient that
was the Soviet Union. The removal of the state regulation of
prices led to a threefold increase in the cost of groceries and
other staples previously sold below their market value or simply
unavailable, like decent quality toilet paper. The resulting
hyperinflation wiped out people's savings practically overnight.
Salaries were delayed, and many pensioners found themselves
begging or selling anything they had at makeshift market stalls.
I remember one such spot very close to Katya's home. Babushkas
sat there on wooden crates during the bitter winter months with
a selection of homemade jams, pickles, home-knitted wool socks
and mittens, tableware and even Second World War medals.
Ordinary Russians associate the 1990s with hardship, uncertainty and ubiquitous crime. Perhaps the best account of that
era is *Secondhand Time*, a book of orally recorded experiences of

human suffering collected by Nobel laureate Svetlana Alexievich. Individual stories hummed by doctors, soldiers, pensioners and retail workers join together in a choir of overwhelming pain and despair at being betrayed by the state. Katya and I lived through those years, which have undoubtedly shaped us.

People like Katya have witnessed first hand how life in Russia has gradually improved since the mid-1990s. She graduated from university around 2000, when Putin became president, and started a career in management and commerce, achieving a substantially higher level of prosperity as an adult than her parents could have ever imagined. Perhaps ordinary people in Russia have not caught up with Western standards of living in terms of disposable income or wealth, but they are much better off than they've *ever* been. People have access to mortgages and other personal loans, and low-income families and pensioners get state support; in addition to free healthcare, private medical services are relatively affordable; it is now common to have cars; everyone has a smartphone; and energy and mobile data are cheap. And everyone aged forty and older still remembers with a shudder the chaos of the 1990s. In the current climate of relative prosperity and stability, people aren't prepared to risk everything to stand up for rights and liberties. Loss aversion is real.

Katya laughs when I bring up strikes. She says that in the West there is a history of civil rights movements. It's completely normal to gather to protest there. 'I sometimes wonder whether people in France work at all,' she chuckles. 'But here it's not like that.'

And, of course, since Vladimir Putin took office, he has been clamping down on any grassroots protests, including more recent arrests that led to especially severe punishments, seemingly at random. This is how you sow terror, I think, but don't say out loud.

It's getting late. Just as we did three decades ago, we have talked for hours taking no notice of the time. I ask one last question.

'What are you personally hoping for, Katya?'

'I very much hope that Russia will be respected not only for its military power, but for its science and technology, sports, arts and culture.'

So do I, Katya. So do I.

Chapter 5

'I Only Scream When I'm Asleep'

Kostya Morozov has straw-blond hair, pale blue eyes and a bit of a paunch. 'Well, Jana, what did you expect?' he says, embracing me. 'I turned fifty last year!' I met Kostya some three decades ago in Sphinx, a legendary Yekaterinburg rock club. Opened in 1993, it was the first post-Soviet space in the city, frequented by young Russians who were excited by the new openness to the West. We would discuss The Cure's new album, and listen to Agatha Christie, Nautilus Pompilius, Chaif and other Yekaterinburg bands. Guys like Kostya came for a beer or two, and stayed until the first tram rumbled by in the morning.

These days, Kostya doesn't go out much. He has a demanding job in logistics. His wife Sveta is an accountant at one of the most prestigious employers in Yekaterinburg – a huge conglomerate with interests in farming, construction, manufacturing and financial services. I am impressed, but Sveta dodges the compliment. 'Jana, this is Russia. I will never make more money than my husband or a male colleague who does the same job as me. Trust me, I run the payroll!' As she says this, still wearing her smart work outfit, she is slicing *sujuk*, cured Armenian beef. The kitchen table, in their lovingly decorated open-plan living room, is already laden with *zakuski*. There are pickled mushrooms with soured cream, gherkins, open sandwiches with marrow caviar, sliced cheese and persimmons. 'It's nothing fancy.'

Meanwhile, Kostya doesn't offer me tea. Instead, he opens the freezer and pours us some vodka. We drink the first shots neat, as is customary. We have not seen each other for many years, but we've kept in touch, primarily because of their only daughter, Nadya.

She took up tennis at age four. That was in summer 2012 after the Morozovs had been watching Wimbledon, and a commentator pointed out Valeria Savinykh, a twenty-one-year-old from Yekaterinburg, who had got through to the second round. In Russia, girls are usually enrolled in artistic gymnastics, figure skating or ballroom dancing. The old chestnut that a girl should be feminine is still stuck in the Russian value system. Perhaps fortunately for Nadya Morozova, she was a strong child rather than dainty. Kostya and Sveta looked up a tennis club in Yekaterinburg and took Nadya along. A coach gave her a racket and threw a ball at her. She hit it back. So that was that.

Three years later, Nadya was training five days a week after school. Kostya was now taking her to a bigger tennis centre on the other side of town. Nadya has been staying up until nine or ten at night doing her homework for as long as she can remember. Sveta and Kostya became tennis parents, accompanying their daughter to regional and national championships and sending her to summer tennis schools in Georgia and Armenia, because that was cheaper than training in Sochi, the 'Russian California' by the Black Sea. Nadya aspired to play in Europe. When she wasn't practising tennis, she studied English with a tutor twice a week during school terms. Her parents kept their heads down and worked hard. The invasion of Ukraine hit their tiny world like a wrecking ball.

Fifteen-year-old Nadya shut herself in her bedroom and wouldn't come out. She refused to eat or go to school. 'What's the point?' she said. 'I'm ashamed to be Russian. And I will never get to play internationally!' There was little her parents could say to console her. One night Kostya called me in London in despair. 'I don't know what to say to her. She is right: we are fucked.' At the time I did what I could and told Nadya about Russian people who were taking food to those detained for anti-war demonstrations, lawyers who worked pro bono to get them released, Russians in Europe who donated money to buy medical supplies for people in Ukraine and activists who lobbied Western governments to put pressure on the Kremlin with asset freezes and travel bans. I could have told her about Russian women who ran shelters for victims of domestic violence, something which had spiked since the launch of the so-called 'Special Military Operation', but I stopped there. Violent crime targeting women all over Russia, committed by traumatised military personnel returning from the war zone, has been documented by various independent human rights organisations.[1] It is not being discussed by the mainstream media; such allegations could

---

1. According to the analysis by Vot Tak, in the period from 1 January to 4 September 2024, war veterans killed seven women and five children (as well as three men). Six women and three girls were raped, including an eleven-year-old girl from the Urals. Vot Tak also reports fourteen assaults. It is impossible to estimate the number of crimes that do not get reported.

potentially be interpreted as 'discrediting' the Russian army. Instead, I told Nadya to go hit some balls. I don't know whether my words helped. I only know that every one of us had to find a way out of that state of apathy and helplessness. For Nadya, it was tennis.

Nadya's parents explain that she is currently in Yerevan for a tournament as we raise a toast to her. International competitions were banned in Russia in early 2022, but a player, even a junior one, must participate in international tournaments if they hope to get ranked.

'We knew from the outset that tennis was going to be expensive, but living it is another reality,' says Sveta. 'We are spending 100,000 rubles (c. £833) a month on tennis, and that doesn't include travel.' 'We don't have that kind of money to keep supporting her,' chimes in Kostya. 'The Russian tennis federation doesn't help.'

'You need an oligarch for a father – then your child has a shot,' says Sveta bitterly. 'If you hear a story about a girl from the armpit of Russia moving up the ranks now that she is training in Mallorca or Cannes (where top European tennis academies are based), you have to ask yourself the question: how can her parents afford that? The average salary in Russia is less than 100,000 rubles a month.'

'It also helps if your parents are former players now coaching children at the national academies,' adds Kostya. 'Then you can revolve the entire tennis school around your child. It happens in Moscow, and it happens here.'

This is why some years ago the Morozovs began to think about sending Nadya to a US university that offers scholarships to talented young athletes. Sveta found an agency, run by a Russian expat in Ohio. In the summer of 2023, the Morozovs recorded a video of Nadya's training session and sent it to the recruiter. Within a month, they had received a dozen full scholarship offers from US universities.

'How many offers have you received in total?'

'Twenty-one.'

They have done virtual tours of almost all the campuses, researched university rankings, spoken to tennis coaches and narrowed their choice down to two. In a year's time, Nadya will be studying in the US.

I propose a toast to the talented girl and her parents. They drink, but there is no jubilation. The frowns are back.

Most universities ask for a TEFL (Test of English as a Foreign Language, a standard university admission requirement for students who are non-native speakers of English). Soon after the invasion of Ukraine, TEFL announced it was pulling out of Russia, as if such an act would teach Putin a lesson. Now young hopefuls like Nadya must travel to Georgia, Armenia or Kazakhstan to take the test. This too costs money.

'We have no one to talk to. We haven't even told the grandparents about all the offers Nadya has received.'

I think back to 1996, when, at sixteen years old, I was heading to Germany on a full scholarship, paid for by a private donor whose family had fled Russia after the Bolshevik Revolution. He and his wife have been covering the tuition fees of Russian and Eastern European students for some years, helping hopefuls like me to get educated in some of the most prestigious private schools in Europe. My entire family gathered to see me off. My grandparents had lived through the horrors and hardships of the Second World War, yet they were delighted that their granddaughter was going to a German high school. They were a little anxious about a young girl moving to a foreign country by herself, but I know they were very proud of me and excited about the opportunities ahead. Unlike Nadya, I already had some experience of living abroad with a German host family, in 1994. I knew that I appeared as exotic to Germans as they did to me. When I ate a kiwi unpeeled during a lunchbreak, I became a freak sensation among the high school children, who couldn't believe that someone in their teens could be eating one for the first time. And so, when I enrolled at a boarding school two years later, I wasn't surprised that I struggled to fit in. While the kids of the German elite felt at home within the school castle building, parading around in their Escada dresses and Polo shirts, Russian and Polish students buried themselves in economics books (because of course we all chose to study a subject with a high career potential) and comfort-ate Nutella straight from the jar. While I made few friends there and experienced occasional bullying, I ended up graduating with IB scores that earned me a place at Oxford. I know only too well that Nadya won't find it easy, even in this age of easy online communication, but I also have faith in this tenacious young woman.

'Will you try to speak to your parents about Nadya going abroad?' I ask Sveta.

'Nadya told her grandmother sometime in 2022 that she was thinking of applying to universities in the US. My mother's response was "Over my dead body!"' Sveta's mother was convinced that America was full of 'gays, black people and drug addicts', an unsuitable place for her Russian granddaughter. She voiced her opinion in no uncertain terms, and Nadya came home in tears. Sveta remembers how her mother had once impatiently waited for a samizdat copy of Solzhenitsyn's *The Gulag Archipelago*. Now she reminisces about the Soviet Union. Sveta asks her, 'What was so good about it?' Her mother replies, 'We used to be able to leave our house keys under the doormat.' Sveta tells her, 'We had nothing worth stealing! Most Soviet families lived in identical flats with identical furniture and crockery. We didn't have a washing machine or a vacuum cleaner. Carpets on the wall were a sign of prosperity! Do you really want to go back to empty shelves and samizdat?'

When Sveta's mother saw a TV report of Belgorod in the west of Russia being hit by Ukrainian missiles, she was appalled. When her daughter pointed out that this was what Russia had been doing to Ukraine for months, she paused, then repeated the official government line that the Russian military was helping Ukraine to liberate its people from the Nazis. 'Mother! We can't tell people how to live. What if the Chinese take over Russia and start "liberating" us?'

Presently, Sveta asks Kostya to refill her glass. 'When I hear this talk of Nazis or NATO in the office, I end the conversation. I say I'd better get back to work.' She shrugs. 'Most of my colleagues are reasonable people. They say that what's happening is awful, but that there is nothing we can do about it. We also have a security guard who reckons that after Ukraine we should take Turkey too.' Sveta laughs, then takes a large sip of vodka.

'People don't care about the war, and they won't care until their own streets are being shelled. People don't see hardship until they experience it. It's everyone for themselves.'

I ask Kostya about his friends and colleagues at work. He shakes his head. 'You've seen the city, haven't you? The restaurants and bars are full. You can order whatever you want: German beer, French wine, Italian Aperol – you name it. My company is busy and so are many sectors of the economy. I was expecting a slump, but there was none of that. They must have been planning it all for a long time. My boss went on holiday to

Tanzania. Now he is planning to go to Socotra, an expensive island to get to, but you can fly from Yekaterinburg directly to Istanbul or Dubai and then the world is your oyster.'

Sveta sighs. 'We can't even afford to go to Baikal – you probably need 500,000 rubles for that. That's OK. Baikal will get plenty of business from people who work for the security forces or in defence. Those are the new rich.' She pauses and exclaims: '*Pelmeni*! I still need to cook them!' I tell her I'm happy grazing. We refill our glasses.

'Sometimes I wonder whether I'm wrong,' continues Sveta, 'if I should just swim along with the current. They tell us Russia is the greatest country, standing off against the decaying West. Yekaterinburg is thriving as a city: I see cleaned-up streets and parks. Then Nadya comes home and tells me what they teach her at school, and it makes me livid.'

In September 2022, the Russian Ministry of Education introduced weekly 'Important Conversations': mandatory lessons for all schools in Russia. The official website shows the curriculum, which aims to instil 'patriotism', 'loyalty to the Fatherland' and 'traditional family values'. Lessons cover such topics as the inherent greatness of Russia as a country, Russia's role in standing up to the US as the domineering world power, the duty of citizens to defend Russia against foreign invaders, the importance of Russia's nuclear power and the meaning of family values – specifically, traditional heterosexual families who should aim to have as many children as possible. There is a lesson dedicated to the special military forces, including the FSB (Federal Security Service) and their activities, such as spying and sabotage. 'The Reunification of Crimea with Russia' is a lesson in itself, reminding pupils that in 988, Vladimir, the pagan leader of the Kievan Rus', took over Chersonesus, a Greek settlement on the

Crimean Peninsula founded in the sixth century BC. Vladimir agreed to be christened there, a historic event I remember studying at school, which, together with its strategic seaport location, ensured the city's everlasting legacy. During the Tatar-Mongol occupation of Russia in the thirteenth and fourteenth centuries, Crimean settlements were plundered and then abandoned. It was Catherine the Great who had ordered a fortress to be built there in 1783 and founded Sevastopol, still the largest city on the peninsula. This major naval base is a harrowing place in Soviet history, where many thousands lost their lives holding it against the German invasion during the Second World War. The history of Crimea is an integral part of the history of Russia, and of the Soviet Union until its dissolution. I'd be the first to assert that. But in 1991, the former Ukrainian Soviet Socialist Republic, which included Crimea, became a sovereign state. Here the 'Important Conversations' curriculum takes a wild leap, likening the retaking of Sevastopol in 2014 to the heroic battles against the Nazis of 1942.

'Propaganda is all good,' continues Sveta, 'But most people care little about big ideas – they simply want to better their lives. A former colleague of mine went back to her hometown of Kamensk-Uralsky to live closer to her elderly mother. This tiny town has always served the metallurgical industry, and now it has redirected all its production to supply the military. She got a job that pays 70,000 rubles a month, an incredible salary for a provincial town in the Urals. She gets medical insurance, free dental services, free summer camp for the children – it's the peak of aspiration.'

Kostya's parents live in Zarechny, a town of some 20,000 inhabitants east of Yekaterinburg. Their house is not far from a mobilisation centre where men can sign up to join the army.

'They come with their wives and children to fill in the forms. Once they pass the medical, you can see them celebrating with cheap vodka because every new recruit gets about 300,000 rubles on signature and then 180,000 rubles a month. For some people it's ten times their income,' says Kostya. 'They can afford a mortgage and change their family's fortune.'

Sveta insists on cooking *pelmeni*. She fills a pan with water and puts it on a gas stove. She takes me to Nadya's room, which has twenty or thirty trophies displayed on the shelves and as many medals hanging on the walls from singles and doubles tournaments. Otherwise, it's a teenage girl's bedroom with framed photos, plush toys, books and journals. I see that Sveta is already missing her daughter.

She sits down on her bed and says, 'I want Nadya to see the world. I hope she travels all over the States, goes to Mexico, Argentina and Canada. She needs to see the world with her own eyes and make her own conclusions. With fluent English and a decent education, she'll have lots of options.' Sveta falls silent, but she is smiling. 'If she comes back and says, "Mama, America is shit! Europe is shit! Yekaterinburg is the centre of the world," I'll tell her, "Fair enough."' She grins at me. 'But at least she'll have the experience to make that choice.'

Before we return to the living room, I ask Sveta what else she wants for her daughter. 'I want her to be happy.'

Back by the stove, Sveta dips frozen *pelmeni* into boiling water. I open the door to the balcony to get a view of the city at night. I can hardly recognise it, with its new residential buildings where old wooden houses once stood and its bright lights shining with possibilities. But here, despite the comforts of modern development, Russia is turning in on itself.

Eating hot *pelmeni* with cool soured cream, Sveta tells me

about a friend she confided in about their plans to send Nadya abroad. The friend had said, 'Talented children shouldn't be leaving Russia. Who will help raise the country?' Sveta replied that since Nadya hadn't dropped Russia, it shouldn't be up to her to lift it up.

We talk about the curtailment of freedoms over the last decade. In 2013, the Russian State Duma approved legislation to protect minors from 'propaganda of non-traditional sexual relationships', otherwise known as the 'anti-gay laws'. In 2022, this legislation was extended to cover all age groups. Gender re-assignment surgery was banned a year later. At the end of 2023, LGBT+ organisations were declared 'extremist' in Russia.

In 2017, President Putin signed an amendment that decriminalised 'moderate' domestic violence, making it an administrative rather than a criminal offence. It meant that beatings of spouses or children that caused bruising or bleeding, but not broken bones, were punishable by just a fine or, at most, fifteen days in prison, so long as they didn't happen more often than once a year. Previously, such offences carried a jail sentence of up to two years regardless.

The first restrictions on political assemblies were imposed in June 2004 and various subsequent laws made it nearly impossible to protest in Russia. For example, meetings could no longer take place near cultural or educational facilities, near shopping centres or in parks. In 2014, the state introduced criminal liability for repeated violation of the Law of Assemblies, with a punishment of up to five years in prison. Any spontaneous protests in Russia have been brutally dispersed by armed police with their organisers arrested or participants beaten up, detained and fined. In January 2021, fifty-four-year-old Margarita Yudina joined a demonstration in St. Petersburg in support of the arrested opposition leader, Alexei Navalny. She asked the policemen why they were taking a young protester away. In response, she was kicked in the stomach, fell back, fractured her skull and ended up in intensive care. The incident was recorded on someone's phone and widely distributed. The police brutality during the January 2021 protests in Moscow and St. Petersburg was unprecedented in its extremity. It was also deliberate.

We drink in silence.

'We don't have friends with whom we can talk about this,' says Kostya. 'A cousin of mine used to send me messages about Russia's territorial gains in Ukraine, derogatory memes, pseudo-patriotic messages and the like. I blocked him.'

'I keep quiet, but inside I'm weeping,' says Sveta.

I ask them what the word 'patriot' means to them. 'I was born in Russia, I am proud of it,' offers Sveta. 'I love my country. It's the head office that I can't stand.' Kostya says that being a patriot is not being ashamed to say, 'I am Russian.'

I ask about the war.

Kostya says that many people seem to have changed their mind about it over time. At the beginning some discussed the absurdity of the argument that the 'Special Military Operation' was in fact an act of self-defence to pre-empt a NATO invasion. Now people accept that the war is happening so 'we might as well get the job done'. It would be inconceivable for Russia to lose face. Rightly or wrongly, people feel, Russia must prevail.

'Ukraine can't win,' says Sveta, a pained expression clouding her face. 'How can it? Russia has more people, more weapons and more resources to invest in this war. It will stretch for years. Even if Putin dies, his successor will be much the same. The Kremlin will replace him with Ivanov, Petrov or Sidorov – mark my words, it will be a man – and nothing will change.'

'Nothing at all,' echoes Kostya.

'Sometimes I watch Putin on TV, and I wonder how people swallow everything he says. Remember how they explained Prigozhin's plane crash?'

Former convicted thief and gang member Yevgeny Prigozhin used to sell hot dogs on the street before expanding his business ventures to restaurants, food retail and catering, famously serving such foreign dignitaries as Jacques Chirac and George W. Bush. He met Putin in St. Petersburg in the early 1990s and became part of his 'inner circle' by the early 2000s, with his catering business winning numerous government contracts, including the provision of meals to the Russian army. Prigozhin founded a private military company called the Wagner Group, initially to support the separatists in the Donbas area of Ukraine in 2014. Later, Wagner played a part in Russia's actions in the Middle East and Africa, conveniently distancing the Russian government from its involvement in those military theatres. In 2022, after the initial 'Special Military Operation' to 'capture Kyiv in three days' didn't go to plan, the Wagner Group was given the resources and the go-ahead to enlist mercenaries, including prison inmates, to fight in Ukraine. Taking advantage of Putin's disappointment with his state generals, Prigozhin rose to prominence and reportedly became Putin's closest confidant. But the sixty-year-old maverick wasn't a yes-man. He took to social media to criticise the Ministry of Defence, complain about ammunition supply shortages and even attack the luxurious lifestyle of the sons of Russia's top officials, who live in the West and shirk Russian conscription. Prigozhin was becoming a popular household name in Russia, even overshadowing Putin himself despite never earning an official government role or getting state media airtime. In mid-June 2023, the Wagner Group was ordered to integrate itself within the Ministry of Defence. Prigozhin refused.

On 23 June 2023, he released a video claiming that the government's justifications for invading Ukraine were based on falsehoods, and that Russian generals were trying to enrich themselves and deceive Putin and the general public, concealing, among other things, the true number of Russian casualties in the war. The next morning, Prigozhin and his men crossed from Eastern Ukraine into Russia and advanced towards Moscow. They were greeted with cheers on the streets of Rostov-on-Don. Putin made a statement accusing Prigozhin of treason, while the rebel was careful to blame Putin's generals and never the president himself. By the end of that day, thanks to mediation by Belarusian President Alexander Lukashenko, Prigozhin halted his march. He was never prosecuted for his actions and agreed to withdraw his forces from Ukraine, focusing instead on training Belarusian soldiers and conducting operations in Africa. On 23 August 2023, Prigozhin's plane, travelling from Moscow to St. Petersburg, crashed, killing him and nine others on board. Following an official investigation, Putin made an announcement in October 2023 that the crash had been caused by a hand grenade that had detonated inside the aircraft. He also said that alcohol and cocaine had been discovered on board, alluding to the fact that things had got out of hand.

'Case closed!' says Kostya.

'I hate this government, this war and what they are teaching our children. I don't want to be quiet about it, but they've silenced us,' says Sveta. 'I only scream when I'm asleep.'

The picture they paint is so bleak, I am lost for words. I see this family staking everything on a brighter future for their daughter – isolated and in survival mode, browsing shiny websites of university campuses, hoping Nadya will find herself in a world so marvellously different from their own reality.

Sveta is worried that once Nadya goes to the States, she might not be able to see her daughter for a long time. 'What if they close the borders? What if the US stops issuing visas to Russians?' She turns away and wipes her eyes. Kostya refills our glasses. We drink without toasting.

Chapter 6

Suspended Hope

The next morning is crisp with a few wispy clouds suspended in the sky. I walk towards the city centre, hoping that the cool air will help clear my head. Once again, I'm marvelling at how much Yekaterinburg has changed even since my last visit. For the past two decades, I have been mostly keeping abreast of life in the city via social media. Gradually, many of my Yekaterinburg friends created accounts on Facebook and Instagram sharing their own news as well as posts by local media outlets. In 2018, I watched the unfinished television tower from the 1980s being demolished on a Facebook live stream. In 2019, I followed the story of a small park by the Drama Theatre that was supposed to make way for a new church before citizens protested. Several thousand people gathered every night for a week to save the park and, despite initial Kremlin disapproval and arrests, they prevailed. I cheered at these social media posts, because by 2019 successful civic action in Russia had become a rarity. But no news from Yekaterinburg was as informative or entertaining as the posts by Yevgeny Roizman.

Roizman served as mayor of Yekaterinburg from 2013 to 2018. Dressed in jeans and a T-shirt, he ran against the polls' favourite United Party candidate and won, largely due to his popular anti-establishment appeal. A Yekaterinburg native who left home at fourteen, Roizman served a three-year sentence for burglary. Once released, he got a job as a machinist at the Uralmash engineering plant and enrolled in night school, later graduating as a historian and archivist. His rehabilitation experience inspired him to found the 'City Without Drugs' initiative in 1999, a controversial yet effective programme that carried out vigilante-style raids against drug dealers and captured addicts, keeping them locked up until they kicked the habit. Roizman famously addressed criticisms of his 'tough love' campaign by stating that it worked. Having curtailed the drug epidemic in Yekaterinburg, he was ready to roll up his sleeves to tackle other problems in the city, but with the city council and the regional government dominated by United Russia, he found it hard to effect change.

In 2018, as part of the tightening authoritarian regime, the Kremlin abolished mayoral elections in Russia in favour of appointing its own candidates. In response, Roizman resigned and committed himself full-time to writing and charitable and community initiatives. A member of the Academy of Arts and of the Writers Union, Roizman published a dozen books on the history of icon art in the Urals, collections of poems and short stories and an account of his community surgeries and his fight against drugs. The Roizman Foundation, a charity he founded in 2015, raises money to help low-income families in difficult situations – for example, to pay for expensive medical treatment or legal aid. The foundation has helped hundreds of children through social media fundraising campaigns. Its website publishes annual accounts of income and expenses, a level of transparency in stark contrast to most Russian civil servants, who declare their modest incomes and possessions in Russia while concealing villas in Tuscany and fabulous wealth in Western offshore accounts. Roizman's posts on Facebook reminded me of *The West Wing*. He has always inspired a great deal of hope.

Over time, Roizman emerged as one of the Kremlin's most vocal critics. He trolled Kremlin politicians on social media, delighting his followers with his articulate profanities. He ardently supported Alexei Navalny. They enjoyed each other's company. When Navalny came to Yekaterinburg, Roizman challenged him to go for a run. In one of his YouTube videos, Navalny said that he could hardly keep up with the man almost fifteen years his senior. Running has always been Roizman's passion. Every weekend he invited citizens of Yekaterinburg to join him for a jog alongside the embankment, promising tea and cakes afterwards. For more serious runners he launched the very first Europe–Asia Marathon, a race from the city centre to the obelisk, which marks the border between the two continents; it grew into a popular series of year-round running events in the region.

In 2022, Roizman condemned Russia's full-scale invasion of Ukraine and was arrested, accused of 'discrediting' the Russian Armed Forces. He pleaded not guilty and got away with fines. But in August 2022, Roizman was placed under house arrest, banned from using social media, the internet, his telephone and from attending public events. At his trial the following year, he was given a suspended sentence and fined again. Unlike other prominent political activists like Vladimir Kara-Murza and Ilya Yashin, who were imprisoned on similar 'discreditation' charges, Roizman received a much more lenient treatment, but it came at a price. While

Kara-Murza and Yashin were still posting messages on social media from behind bars via their lawyers, Roizman had been gagged. The suspended sentence also marked the end of his weekend runs along the embankment, his community surgeries and his open and honest social media posts. I felt the void even in London.

Still, Roizman stayed in Russia. During his trial, he said, 'I am bound to this place. I was born and bred here. I won't move even a millimetre. Why would I go? I love my country. I understand all the risks, but I can't leave because that would be running away. I cannot allow myself to do that.'

I tried to meet Yevgeny Roizman while I was in Yekaterinburg. I asked a friend with connections in the media to help me get in touch with him, but he couldn't – or wouldn't. I tried not to show my disappointment, but I understood: I may not be an accredited journalist like the *Wall Street Journal*'s Evan Gershkovich, who was arrested in Yekaterinburg in early 2023 on charges of espionage, but in my friend's eyes I still represented an 'unfriendly state'. He was being cautious. I considered trying to find another way to get in touch with Roizman, but ultimately I decided against that. I didn't want to give the authorities any excuse to make his life harder than it already was.

Instead, I decided to visit the Nevyansk Icon Museum, opened in 1999 by Roizman to share his remarkable collection of some 700 local icons. It was the first private icon museum in Russia and remains one of only two. I was told Roizman is often here, greeting visitors and answering questions. I wasn't so lucky, but the museum's collection astonishes me.

In the middle of the seventeenth century, when Patriarch Nikon introduced the liturgical reforms to align the Russian Orthodox Church with the Greek, many Old Believers who resisted the changes came to the Urals to escape the purges. The industrial magnates the Demidovs, who weren't Old Believers themselves, employed new settlers in their ore mining and processing plants and let their labourers practise their religion in private without repercussions. The region prospered.

One of central settlements in the middle of the Urals was Nevyansk, where some families could afford to commission new icons for their homes. The masters passed down their art from one generation to the next, embellishing their fine work with local semiprecious gemstones such as malachite and jasper. Later, gold was discovered in the Urals, and artists took icon art to the next level, by using gold plating and ornaments ordered by the more prosperous local families. Both the masters and their customers worked and dealt in secret. They never protested against the reformed liturgy in public or showed their opposition. But they lived a double life, preserving their faith, traditions and art for generations.

The history of the family icons that survived persecutions throughout the centuries, from Nikon to Stalin, makes me think of my friends in Yekaterinburg who keep themselves to themselves at work and in public but have another life at home, reading banned media sources, discussing politics and bringing up their children with liberal and democratic values.

At the museum shop, there is a selection of books on the history of icon art and the history of the Urals. Those written by Roizman are wrapped in brown paper and labelled with a sticker: 'THIS MESSAGE (MATERIAL) WAS CREATED AND (OR) DISTRIBUTED BY A FOREIGN MEDIA OUTLET, PERFORMING THE FUNCTIONS OF A FOREIGN AGENT, AND (OR) A RUSSIAN LEGAL ENTITY, PERFORMING THE FUNCTIONS OF A FOREIGN AGENT.' Since December 2022, one has not needed to receive funding from abroad to be labelled a 'foreign agent' – being deemed to be 'under foreign influence' is enough. Roizman was put on the register in November 2022. It means that he can no longer organise public events, donate to political candidates, apply for financial support from the state, or teach or produce any content intended for children. At the time of writing, in addition to a couple of hundred organisations, more than 400 individuals are on the register of 'foreign agents' in Russia.

'He is not here,' I text Vera, my old classmate. 'I'll see you soon.' Vera didn't see the point of me trying to meet Roizman in person. While she agrees that he has done a lot for underprivileged people of Yekaterinburg and the Sverdlovsk region, she doesn't see him as a leader. 'He is a controversial figure.' Apart from his vigilante approach to fighting drug crime, Roizman is also rumoured to have been associated with the city's mafia in the 1990s. He does not deny it. Roizman worked in Uralmash, the hot spot of organised crime at the time, where he had presumably met some of the gang members. When asked about his 'City Without Drugs' in interviews, he said that they took any help they could get, including from various crime gangs in Yekaterinburg.

'A leader should be uniting, not dividing people,' says Vera, and she has a point. Misha isn't a fan either: 'As the mayor of Yekaterinburg, Roizman didn't achieve much, or perhaps it would be more accurate to say that he wasn't allowed to. In any case, as a political figure he is yesterday's man.'

I meet Vera for a street-art tour of Yekaterinburg. In recent years, self-appointed tour guides have become popular here, offering art and history walking tours advertised via Telegram. Yekaterinburg's street art, which first appeared in the 1990s, has developed into the largest contemporary art movement in Russia, with an annual festival, called Stenograffia, attended by visitors from all over the country and beyond. Incredibly, we are being shown murals by Spanish and Finnish artists, and there is a trademark balloon piece depicting the space race by English artist Fanakapan. The murals show witches, foxes, horses, clowns and embracing lovers. Again, it's a world away from reality.

Our tour stops in front of a shed painted as the inside of a Yekaterinburg metro carriage. In the centre of the mural a man in black stands behind a woman wearing a crop top, blue jeans and white trainers. He is looking down; she is looking straight ahead, holding on to the rail. The guide asks if we might recognise them. 'Navalnys!' Others look at me in doubt. 'Perhaps,' says the guide, and we continue the tour.

'Protest art! Resistance!' I whisper to Vera.

'What resistance?' she replies. 'It's just a mural.'

Back in Vera and Misha's flat, we sit around a kitchen table with cups of hot tea. They listen politely to my enquiries about whether there are any grassroots initiatives to resist the war or the regime itself, but they only shake their heads. They remind me about Belarus, where over 100,000 people came out to protest the results of the 2020 presidential elections, widely believed to be fraudulent. Alexander Lukashenko declared victory and extended his twenty-six-year reign with a sixth term. In the months that followed, several thousand dissidents were arrested as part of the government crackdown and many were tortured. More than a thousand political prisoners remain locked up in Belarus today. A cautionary tale.

'People in Russia,' they repeat to me patiently, 'are busy with their own lives. Most have got used to the war, which is so far removed from their daily pursuits.' Misha refills my cup as he repeats the word 'resistance'. He says that he doesn't even recall hearing or reading it anywhere other than in the context of

Ukrainians fighting back. 'Most people here have accepted what is happening to them as reality, to which there is no alternative. We don't discuss the war or presidential elections. We care about local flooding, forest fires, dilapidated buildings that need to be taken down before they collapse. The only example of resistance I've heard of is "Idite Lesom".'

Shortly after the September 2022 partial mobilisation announcement in Russia, anti-war activist Grigory Sverdlin founded an organisation that helps Russian men dodge the draft. Its name, Idite Lesom, literally means 'go via the forest' (it is also an idiom for 'go fuck yourself'). In two years it has helped over 37,500 people, including more than 1,000 deserters, hide or leave the country to avoid taking part in the war against Ukraine. It even mobilised lawyers, psychologists, IT engineers and others to help answer 200 to 250 daily queries online. Sverdlin, who left Russia for Georgia in March 2022 because of his own anti-war stance, was previously director of Nochlezhka ('little shelter'), a charity offering social, legal and financial aid to homeless people in Moscow and St. Petersburg. Idite Lesom is crowdfunded and has more of a guerrilla feel than his previous work with the homeless. Still, it does more to prevent shots being fired in Ukraine than any other act of resistance from inside Russia or globally. When asked why it is helping Russians escape rather than mobilising to take down Putin, Sverdlin said that he had seen enough brutally disbanded protests in St. Petersburg in the last decade to realise that it is impossible to hope for change from within. Commenting on his life in self-imposed exile, Sverdlin said that he had had to learn to live with complete uncertainty every single day. He found it surprisingly easy. It's living without a drop of optimism that he could not get used to.

*

After I get back home, I find interviews with Yevgeny Roizman on YouTube. In August 2022, when asked to comment on his position by journalist Katerina Gordeeva, he was characteristically blunt: 'I can't be bothered to get locked up.' Then he gets serious. He talks about good people being tested today: 'Things happen, you stay mum here, you compromise there, there is always a valid reason to switch on survival mode. In these circumstances, remaining true to yourself becomes a task in itself, if not your life's purpose.'

Away from politics, Roizman continues his work on Old Believers icon art in the Urals, hoping to find traces of artists who had kept painting well into the Soviet years. He recently found evidence that some artists were reported to the authorities and executed in the 1930s. He discovered school doors and furniture made from icons confiscated from churches, which had been disassembled or burnt. In all his interviews, Roizman comes across as someone genuinely passionate about his work. It's his personal place of retreat. At the same time, his charitable foundation keeps helping families in need. 'My consolation is that I still do something for individual people, I still make a difference, and this is what matters to me.' In April 2025, a court in Yekaterinburg ruled to shut down the Roizman Foundation on the grounds of financial and operational mismanagement. In response, Roizman vowed that they would appeal and find a way to continue their work.

And people keep coming to him. He tells them not to give up: 'If you can't do anything to change the way things are, maybe you can at least not participate in it.' He knows, of course, that many state employees are told to vote for United Russia candidates in elections and are required to send a photo of their 'correctly' ticked ballots from the voting stations. Teachers are made to teach the Kremlin doctrine to schoolchildren. Paediatricians, making home visits to see sick children, are to ignore grieving mothers who have lost their husbands in the war with Ukraine.

A religious man, Roizman refers to the Bible. 'Evil is winning today. People are losing their faith. It's devastating. It's as if many people have been enchanted over the last twenty years. And I think it will take a long time to unravel this.'

At the end of the interview, Gordeeva, who was declared a 'foreign agent' by the Russian government just a month later in September 2022, asks Roizman what he would choose: homeland or verity. He is silent for a moment. She elaborates, 'Sometimes you need to leave your homeland to stay true to yourself, and sometimes you need to choose your family and your home over your principles. What would you choose?' Roizman dodges the question. I pause the video, thinking about the many Russian expats in Europe who have continued to travel back to Russia to see their families. They take what they call a 'pragmatic approach' to the situation. They don't post anything against Putin or the war on social media. They don't donate to help people in Ukraine or to Navalny's Anti-Corruption Foundation. They want their children to see their grandparents in Russia. They go back to Moscow or Volgograd and follow the rules.

Homeland or verity? How would I answer this question? It is so simple to choose the moral high ground while sitting in front of my laptop in London, but would I really choose to go to prison and never see my parents again? I restart the video. 'I cannot tell you what I would choose. It's a difficult question,' says Roizman. 'These days I find there are too many questions I simply don't have answers to. I used to record videos, write posts on social media, talk to the people coming to see me at length, and now I find that I can't. Of course, I want to see a different Russia under a completely different government. But I also understand very well that, like my sentence, my freedom is suspended.'

Chapter 7

'Crimea Is Ours! And Are *You* Ours?'

At breakfast time, my parents watch the *Good Morning* show on television. Like in the West, the programme features news, studio interviews, weather forecasts and infotainment, easily palatable at this time of day. The news on the state-controlled Russian media is never too gruesome, unless there is a school shooting in the US or fatalities following a desperate migrant crossing in the Mediterranean. Reports on activities in Ukraine show drones flying over empty fields with commentary from a newsreader on targeted military strikes, or else an interview with a grateful Russian-speaking Ukrainian from Donetsk, thanking Putin for standing up to Kyiv. The rest of the show is intended to be heart-warming, with a daily feature on regional cuisines, showcasing Buryat dumplings, Tatar flatbreads and elk-meat pasties from Karelia. It's a picture of Russian ethnic diversity on a plate, brought to millions of homes. And, of course, there is a daily horoscope. First appearing as a fad in the early 1990s, horoscopes have become a regular feature of TV and radio shows, newspapers and online news portals. It is a curious development for a country that in Soviet times took pride in its science and technology, economic progress, rationality and atheism.

My father gets up from the table and tells my mother he is off to finish chopping up the fallen birch tree. He doesn't say a word to me, which is fine. The day before he called me a traitor and the biggest disappointment of his life, so I'm not in a talkative mood either.

It wasn't always like this.

In March 1985, when Mikhail Gorbachev took over as the general secretary of the Soviet Politburo, my father was thirty-one years old. He had followed his parents' footsteps into academia and worked in the analytical chemistry lab of the physics faculty at the Ural Polytechnic Institute (now part of the Ural Federal University). A charismatic extrovert by nature, he must have felt depressingly out of place there. Gorbachev's reforms of perestroika (restructuring), glasnost (openness) and *uskoreniye* (acceleration) could not have been more welcomed by my father, who had never joined the Communist Party, despite the obvious advantages it offered in terms of career prospects. He was a rebel: for example, he was one of the organisers of the first ever discotheque held in Sverdlovsk (the Soviet name for Yekaterinburg). Our two-bedroom flat in a 1970s Soviet apartment block might have had the same layout as millions of others, but inside we had posters of ABBA and the Beatles instead of traditional carpets on the walls. When other Soviet citizens pined for a new fridge or a colour TV, my father procured a free roll of malachite-patterned wrapping paper from a confectionery factory and decorated our hallway with it instead of buying wallpaper. In our living room, we had a synthetic carpet on the floor and a black-and-white TV, but we had Solzhenitsyn and Grossman on our bookshelves and piles of literary magazines inside the wall cabinets. Even during Soviet times, my parents managed to join organised group tours to Finland, France, Spain and Italy. When I was about five years old, my father went to Japan and brought me a map of Tokyo's Disneyland and a wind-up Minnie Mouse toy. I adored him.

In 1989, at a conference in Moscow, my father met representatives of Carl Zeiss, an East German optics manufacturer. A year later, he opened a showroom of their microscopes before leaving university and setting up his own import business. He started with lab equipment but diversified into eyewear, second-hand cars, furniture, tableware and apparel. His work took him to Germany, Austria and Switzerland. I was already studying at a school where I was learning English as a foreign language from the age of six. My father encouraged me to study German as well. Europe was the future. My parents, who used to save money to buy an ABBA LP and dream of scoring a denim jacket, were now re-setting their aspirations. We still lived in the same flat, but amid the general hardship of the 1990s, our family did rather well. My father drove a used Mercedes, bought us clothes from German C&A and took us on holiday to Bulgaria. To a child brought up in the Soviet Union, even Eastern Europe was jaw-dropping in its relative abundance. I began to learn German, and in 1994 I stayed with the family of my one of my father's business partners for half a year, attending school and imbibing Western European culture. Back in Russia, I dreamt of going abroad to continue my studies. We never talked about it explicitly at home, but the direction of travel was clear: my future was in the West, and my parents supported me absolutely.

After graduating from the Russian state school in 1996, I received a scholarship to study the International Baccalaureate at a German boarding school. It was another business partner of my father who had helped to open that door. Two years later I applied to study at Oxford. I asked my father to pay for my flight to London to attend the interview. I got in, and after a delay with my visa, caused by Russia's financial crisis, I finally began my degree in Economics and Management in 1999. Afterwards I got a job in London with a US investment bank, which sponsored my visa to remain in the UK. London has become my home. I always felt grateful to my parents for their foresight in enrolling me in one of the best state schools in Yekaterinburg, where I learned English and honed my ambition among equally talented and hardworking kids. I'm convinced that it's thanks to my parents that I grew up valuing intellectual curiosity, caught my travel bug early on and ended up designing my life around London's theatreland, BBC Radio 4 and sharp-minded people. But somewhere in the last twenty years my parents and I have diverged. My previously liberal, avant-garde-loving father and I no longer see eye-to-eye. It is devastating, impossible to accept and difficult to understand. But I must try.

When I try to pinpoint the exact time that my father and I fell out over politics, I always recall an email he sent me straight after the annexation of Crimea. The Kremlin made sure to mark the event with a series of celebrations in Moscow and Crimea itself: the state-controlled TV channels broadcast President Putin's speeches and pop music concerts. Addressing the State Duma in March 2014, Putin said, 'In people's hearts and minds, Crimea has always been an inseparable part of Russia.' The president also condemned the Western reaction to the 'unification', including the proposed economic sanctions against Russia. 'Today,' he said, 'it is imperative to end this hysteria, to refute the rhetoric of the Cold War and to accept the obvious fact: Russia is an independent, active participant in international affairs; like other countries, it has its own national interests that need to be taken into account and respected.' No doubt inspired by the president's address, my father wrote to me saying, 'Crimea is ours! And are *you* ours?'

Some years earlier I had left the City and was working as a freelance corporate finance consultant and broadcaster, running a series of events celebrating inspiring women. Russian politics wasn't exactly on my mind, but events in Ukraine, which began with protests against government corruption in Kyiv's Independence Square, Maidan Nezalezhnosti, in November 2013, were impossible to miss. By that time, many of my school friends from Russia had joined Facebook, a social network I had spent a lot of time on promoting my women's events. Facebook was popular in those days, with any political news often provoking a discussion. I found it striking at the time how the political crisis in Ukraine incited totally opposite reactions from my Western and Russian friends. Whereas Western readers focused on the illegitimacy of the Crimea referendum to join the Russian Federation, many Russians were posting celebratory messages about Russia's strength and unity, while denouncing anyone who disagreed with the Kremlin. They were referred to as 'the fifth column', 'traitors' or 'Western puppets'. There was a lot of angry rhetoric about Ukrainians, all of them condemned as nationalists who wanted to ban the Russian language in Ukraine and 'clean the country of foreign influence'. My father, too, accused me of being unpatriotic for not supporting the 'reunification' of Crimea with Russia. In one heated discussion during a visit in the summer of 2014, he called me a 'traitor' for having Western views. 'It is time for you to leave London and come back to Russia.'

In a way, his views weren't surprising. They reflected what was being broadcast on Russian state television every morning and every night. News and talk shows distorted reality, encouraging rage and hatred. For example, the words 'homosexual' and 'paedophile' were used interchangeably when discussing a child abuse case. News bulletins followed exactly the same script every day: Putin the Wise signing a decree in his royal office, Putin the Brave visiting a far province, while reporting of US news focused on school shootings, natural disasters and political scandals. My parents, who had been exposed to the Kremlin's media for nearly two decades by that time, were repeating the same newspeak to me.

Still, I could not believe that my intelligent, inquisitive and previously rebellious parents had been so duped. Could media propaganda be so strong and effective by itself? It was not until I read *The Invention of Russia* by Arkady Ostrovsky that I understood that propaganda fed not so much on ignorance but on resentment. My father, a once hopeful entrepreneur, who had embraced perestroika and new opportunities of the open economy, had been defeated by the ubiquitous corruption, lack of state support for small businesses, extortionate interest rates and bureaucracy. Forever putting out fires, he was ultimately forced to close his business when he could no longer afford to pay his staff and rent. At sixty, he had a house in the country, built on a plot of land inherited from his father's dacha, but no steady income or savings. His only child was striving to achieve her own fulfilment in faraway London, with no plans to move closer to her ageing parents. It must have been a very challenging set of circumstances to accept, especially for an ambitious and once brilliant man. State broadcasts offered an escape of sorts. They projected the growing strength and importance of the Russian state. The annexation of Crimea gave people like my father a sense of victory and national pride. Being part of the bigger and stronger Russia – a patriotic image concocted by the media – successfully compensated my father for personal failures and disappointments in life.

On the morning of 24 February 2022, I was in my flat in London taking in the news. My TV was on, and I was at my laptop scanning articles, while checking social media posts on my phone. I was still in my pyjamas, and pouring coffee from a cafetiere, hoping I wouldn't miss the cup. I was firing off messages and responding to friends who, like me, were in a state of shock. I also sent an email to the editor at the *Evening Standard* about the article they had commissioned the day before. It was supposed to focus on what ordinary people in Russia and Ukraine had thought about the amassed troops on the border. I had planned to re-read what I had written in the morning before filing. Now I was having to rewrite it. I contacted some people in Yekaterinburg who echoed my own sentiment: anger and shame as well as fear for the future of both of our countries. I kept checking Facebook, at the time still accessible in Russia without a VPN. I expected to see universal condemnation. I pulled up the profiles of those Russian friends who had been supporting Putin. Some were silent, but others were not. They shared the Kremlin's slogans about the 'denazification' of Ukraine and showing solidarity towards our Russian-speaking Ukrainian 'brothers' and 'sisters' who 'needed to be rescued' from Kyiv. I messaged a few. Some were calm and expressed a view that Russia would finally bring peace and prosperity to Eastern Ukraine in the same way it had poured money into Crimea. Others were more aggressive, supporting military action to take Kyiv. I couldn't quite process it all and focused on my article. I had to speak up on behalf of those Russians who, like me, felt angry, helpless and ashamed.

It took some time but, ultimately, I saw my own naivety. In his book *Misbelief,* psychologist and behavioural economist Dan Ariely explains how proponents of conspiracy theories become deeply entrenched in their views as they keep rationalising the world through the same lens – be it the advantages of Brexit, the righteousness of Donald Trump or the perils of vaccination. Once such views are set, their champions become emotionally attached to them, which means that facts, figures or even pictures of destroyed buildings in Mariupol won't help dissuade them from their position. Besides, in the case of Putin's invasion of Ukraine, it is much more comforting to believe that the Kremlin is liberating innocent people from neo-Nazis than to accept that your own people are killing, looting and destroying a neighbouring country. I saw this attitude in my mother. It was much more palatable for her to imagine that someone else was responsible for the ruins of Mariupol than to process that the Russian army was capable of such warrantless destruction. She was frightened. Soon direct air travel between Russia and Europe was no longer possible, Western and liberal media sites and social networks were banned, new sanctions were imposed and the ruble eventually devalued against the dollar and the euro. It was difficult to believe that a government would willingly provoke such a cost at the expense of its own people. Those Russians who had approved of the annexation of Crimea and intervention in Eastern Ukraine doubled down on their support for the full-scale invasion. The rest soon fell silent.

92   THE GOOD RUSSIAN

After speaking to my mother, I knew better than to try
my father. If my apolitical mother was simply repeating the
Kremlin's messages, my father would be amplifying them. His
older sister began sending me derogatory memes, blaming the
West for the invasion and insulting the people of Ukraine. I
asked her to stop, but I couldn't bring myself to call her either.
I thought about their late father, my grandfather, a brilliant historian called Alexander Bakunin. He joined the Soviet Army in
1942 to defend his motherland against Hitler, and now his country was the aggressor. How would he have taken it? After the
end of the Second World War, he came to Yekaterinburg (then
Sverdlovsk) to apply to study history at the Ural State University.
He got his doctorate, researching the economic history of the
industrialisation of Urals in the 1930s. He became head of the
Department of History of the Communist Party of the Soviet
Union at the Ural State Technical University and was also one
of the founders of the Institute of History and Archaeology in
Yekaterinburg. A prolific author, my grandfather was a revered
professor who supervised dozens of doctoral candidates. Some of
them would join our family celebrations for his birthday, always
delivering elaborate speeches to toast his health. Most remarkably, during the era of glasnost, my grandfather turned to the
newly opened archives and began researching the evolution of
totalitarian power in the Soviet Union, mass repression and the
human cost of industrialisation in the Urals. He died of a heart
attack – his fourth – in 1999, having published two books of a
projected trilogy entitled *The History of Soviet Totalitarianism*.

In the 1990s, it didn't feel that significant that an established
professor of history and Communist Party member was rethink-
ing his life's labour. At the time, that was the preoccupation
for many. It is only now, when newly erected busts and statues

of Stalin are popping up all over Russia, that I find my grandfather's academic humility so admirable. I wish I could talk to
him right now.

When I was little, I spent at least a month every summer at my
grandparents' dacha. Both of my grandparents would be busy
all day, tending to tomatoes and cucumbers in the greenhouse,
weeding berries, herbs, peas and root vegetables, making fire-
wood for the furnace and doing many other chores. Grandfather
was also an avid berry and mushroom picker, and my grandmother made jams and pickled mushrooms to last all winter.
While my grandmother had grown up in the city, her husband
thrived in nature. He loved hunting and fishing and made sure to
spend time in the country all year round. After dinnertime, my
grandfather liked sitting outside by the fire. He would kindle it
with an old newspaper and some birch bark and send me to the
forest to bring back a few dried branches to add to a log or two.
Then we would sit staring at the flames in silence. I didn't mind
that at all, grateful I was allowed to stay up late and keep him
company. As a child, I couldn't possibly imagine what he used to
think about on those warm summer nights. But I think I do now.

We had always believed that my grandfather was born and
raised in Tundrino, a small village on the Ob River in the Surgut
region of Western Siberia. Before the Bolshevik Revolution,
Tundrino was home to a brick manufacturing plant and a fishing business, both owned by a merchant named Kositsyna, who
also ran a fish deli in Moscow. Both were nationalised by the
Soviet state in 1918, and from what I knew, my great-grandfather
and his older sons had worked at that fishing *kolkhoz* (a Soviet
collective enterprise). My grandfather Alexander was the
youngest, and he was conscripted after he had finished studying at a local college in the hope of becoming a teacher. After

demobilisation, he briefly returned to Siberia and then came to Sverdlovsk in the Urals, ostensibly driven by his ambition to earn a history degree from a prestigious university. He met my grandmother at the same university, and this was how they settled in Sverdlovsk, which had its old name, Yekaterinburg, reinstated in the 1990s.

Sometime during the pandemic, my father took up genealogy, hoping to trace his family tree. He made a harrowing discovery. It turned out that his father was born in Smirnovo, in the Dalmatov district of Shadrinsk (now Kurgan) region of the Ural Mountains, about 200 km to the west of Yekaterinburg. The family's name was Bakulin with an 'l'. Bakulins had lived in the Urals for generations – certainly since the 1710s, when the surname was recorded in a census conducted by a local monastery. Later, more detailed entries suggest that the family came to the Urals from Kokshengsky Stan, an ancient Slavic settlement on the fertile lands between the Kokshenga and Vaga rivers in the north-east of Russia. Our forefathers arrived when many Old Believers migrated to the area to escape persecution following the 1652–66 Russian Orthodox Church reforms. They may have even been Old Believers themselves. Two centuries later, under the Soviets, the Bakulin family in Smirnovo was branded *kulaks* – prosperous peasants who were considered class enemies. Lenin referred to them as 'bloodsuckers' and 'profiteers', declaring them targets of the revolution. Officially, *kulaks* were the owners of over three hectares of land and plenty of livestock, but in reality, anyone with a cow and a tidy plot of land could have been labelled 'the enemy' in 1920s–30s Russia. In 1930, my great-grandparents and their four children, including five-year-old Alexander, were rounded up along with other relatively well-off peasants and deported to Siberia. It is hard to imagine what it must have been like to disembark on the bank of the River Ob and be told to start digging.

Some years ago I read a fascinating novel: *Zuleikha* by Guzel Yakhina. It narrates the exile of a peasant woman who was taken from her small Tatar village in the south of Russia and sent to Siberia in 1930, along with other 'enemies of Soviet power'. They are dropped off on a riverbank and left to settle in. They make a *zemlyanka*, a hole dug in the ground with a makeshift roof – a primitive dwelling made to survive long, harsh winters. They struggle. The woman gives birth but she doesn't have any milk, so she cuts her fingers and feeds her baby droplets of blood. Yakhina's novel is a work of fiction, but it draws on the lived experience of her grandmother, who survived the Gulag. Its vivid narrative gave me a sense of what my own great-grandparents and their children had to endure in the Surgut region on the Ob, with its short summers, cold winters and untamed taiga.

The Bakulin family survived. They even thrived. All four siblings, Mikhail, Ivan, Alexander and his older sister Faina, fought in the Second World War. Their duty and sacrifice helped them distance themselves somewhat from their tarnished background as the children of *kulaks*. But it wasn't enough, because their passports would have still betrayed their status as class enemies. After demobilisation, Alexander returned to Siberia and first worked as a village teacher before enrolling to study at a pedagogical institute in Tyumen. People of their status weren't meant to enter higher education, so someone must have helped Alexander. When he arrived in Sverdlovsk hoping to transfer to Ural State University, his passport said 'Alexander Bakunin', with an 'n'. It was clean. At first, he wasn't successful in getting in because the student dorms were full, but he appealed to the institution's deputy head, who had a reputation for being sympathetic to war veterans. Alexander graduated in 1951 with flying colours.

He was assigned to the Ural Polytechnic Institute (later, Ural State Technical University) where he joined the Communist Party. This was not a matter of choice for an aspiring academic. His place of work was literally called the Department of History of the Communist Party of the Soviet Union. Gradually, he built a successful career. He married my grandmother, who taught chemistry at the same university, and they had two children. In time, the Bakunins received their own flat in the city centre near the university and bought a Volga car. The flat boasted a spacious reception room with crystal glassware and fine Soviet porcelain. They had a decent-sized kitchen with a large window and two bedrooms, one of which became my grandfather's study after my aunt and father had flown the family nest. Brimming with books, the study's wall cabinets were also decorated with photos of my grandfather posing with colleagues in Moscow, Dushanbe and Tashkent. A respected academic, he could also afford trips to the Soviet spa in Kislovodsk, which he and my grandmother visited many times. In the early 1960s, when the regional government granted land to Sverdlovsk academics for their recreational use in the summer, my grandparents got 600 square metres (just under 6,500 square feet) of land in a beautiful place called Flyus, surrounded by birch and pine forests, some 40 km from Sverdlovsk. They were permitted to build a summer cottage and plant apple trees. This became our beloved family dacha, where I spent most of my summers with my grandparents, aunt, uncle, parents and cousin Dima.

The memories of my childhood – my flared-trousers-wearing parents, my immaculately permed grandmother, my aunt with her customary red lipstick and my grandfather, proudly at the wheel of his treasured Volga, taking the family back into town at the end of the summer – at least four of us squeezed into the back seat, together with a Pekingese and a cat, bags of homegrown vegetables and herbs on our knees – are impossible to reconcile with the unimaginable hardship of Alexander's own early years. It doesn't help that until recently none of us knew anything about our ancestors being uprooted and sent to Siberia. Of his children, wife and colleagues, none had any idea about the true origins of our family history.

My father recalls how his father used to take him fishing or hunting in the Kurgan region of the Urals. He had no idea that the area might have had a significance to him. They never went to Smirnovo, though – at least not together. On these trips, my grandfather would tell his son about fishing in the Ob, hunting and picking pinecones. He mentioned hunger and hardship in the early 1930s but was never specific. My grandmother, my father and my aunt all went to visit Alexander's parents in Siberia while they were still alive. They had moved 600 km south to Yalutorovsk, a small town near Tyumen in Eastern Siberia, which was much closer to Smirnovo (250 km – a trivial distance by Russian standards) than it was to Tundrino. But no one in the family ever suspected the closely guarded secret my grandfather took to his grave.

It is obvious why he hid the truth during the communist era; *kulaks* were as viciously portrayed as aristocrats in Soviet history textbooks. According to Soviet ideology, all of its citizens came from the 'worker and peasant' class. My grandfather built a new life for himself and his family precisely because he was able to conceal his tainted past. It is more difficult to understand why the wave of glasnost in the late 1980s and 1990s didn't lead him to open up about the events of his early childhood. I should mention that Grandfather never talked about the war either. Perhaps he simply put the past behind him with the intention of never rummaging through his horrible memories. That generation kept private things to themselves. But when it came to his work, he *did* bravely rewrite history. The times were changing: sealed archives were opened to historians for the first time, journalism became cool and the mass media cast the old propaganda aside and broadcast with unprecedented candour. Nevertheless, old institutions, including academia, weren't marching along at the same pace. It must have been a real act of will for my grandfather to re-examine the past with a radical lens. In the first two volumes of *The History of Soviet Totalitarianism* (1996 and 1997), he reconstructed previously concealed facets of the Soviet regime: violence, lawlessness and abuse of power. He used the term 'genocide' to describe the famine caused by collectivisation and argued that repression was used against middle-class peasants to induce them and poorer folk into joining collective farms. One of his former students, Raissa Moskvina, writes that 'even after the collapse of the regime, one needed to overcome "the internalised Bolshevik", the "Soviet mentality", the outside pressure, especially in academia, and the fear. One never knew how long the period of thaw would last.' She says that *The History of Soviet Totalitarianism* was Alexander Bakunin's most important work. Her take is part of a book of essays, *Alexander Vasilievich Bakunin Remembered* (2004), penned by his colleagues and students, published after his death. Incredibly – or maybe less so in hindsight – hardly anyone else mentions his work on totalitarianism at all. Perhaps historians saw that the liberal tide wasn't here to stay and remained prudently silent.

In her tribute, Moskvina postulates that digging into 'the permafrost of Russian unfreedom' might have cut Alexander

Bakunin's life short. 'Researching the Gulag and mass repressions, Bakunin focused his attention on ruined human fates, and it weighed heavily on his heart. For he wrote from his heart.' Gennadiy Shveikin, a prominent chemist and Grandfather's friend and neighbour in Flyus, recalled reading the first two volumes, respectively on the genesis and the apogee of totalitarianism in Russia. They had astonished him. He told my grandfather that there should be a third book on how to help Russia process its past and find a path towards a different future. His friend said that he was working on it already. In April 1999, my grandfather died of a heart attack while using a cast-iron bar to strike hard ice in front of his garage. 'It must have been an unbearable task – to break up the ice of our history.'

I'm sitting at a dining room table in my aunt's living room. It's eleven in the morning. My aunt dishes out a plate of sliced vegetables and herbs, cheese, a grated beetroot salad generously dressed with garlic mayonnaise, dark rye bread and still-hot fried mushroom pasties. My aunt, now in her seventies, puts on her trademark red lipstick. My grandfather's favourite student and long-time friend of my aunt, Ekaterina Zakharova, is here too. Also in her seventies, she is a busy entrepreneur who has come for a quick visit. We raise a toast to my grandfather and drink our vodka shots. I wince and chuckle as I see myself through the eyes of a Westerner now able to legitimately confirm their stereotypical view of Russians, drinking vodka in the morning. Hey, reader, I've had only a mouthful! Besides, we have not seen each other for a long time. My aunt and father have shared their views on the family past with me already. Both think that their father and his siblings made a pact to take the secret to their graves. It's possible, if a little dramatic. Ekaterina has a slightly different view.

'Your grandfather was an extraordinary man. He was a prominent historian, an incredible leader and teacher. We all called him
'Teacher' with a capital 'T'. He was larger than life.' Her phone
rings, but she silences it. 'My parents too were purged *kulaks*, and
it wasn't a big deal because times were changing, and also, I was
a nobody in comparison to your grandfather. He had to protect
his family and everything he had achieved. He loved you. Do you
know how proud he was of you getting into Oxford?'

'But what about afterwards? He could have told us later.'

Ekaterina reaches out to her bag, looking for a packet of cig-
arettes. 'I can't help it,' she says, dropping the bag. 'I quit years
ago, but I still do that. A lifelong habit.' She drains another shot
instead.

I nod in understanding.

My father has finished chopping up the fallen tree and brought
the logs home. I carry them to a shed, where I climb into the attic
and stack them loosely so they can dry. It's a repetitive task that
gives me time to think. I wonder how my grandfather's secret
might have influenced my father. He grew up in a family of
respected academics who had enviable central accommodation
and other privileges, like access to university-affiliated summer
camps. My father was a straight-A student who went on to study
chemistry at the same institution where both of his parents
worked. His father had a car. When my parents got married,
my grandfather helped them buy a flat and furniture. My father
didn't grow up rich – not by Western or even Soviet standards –
but he enjoyed a cushioned childhood and never had any reason
to question the righteousness of the Soviet state.

I think of Vera and her family. She grew up differently, having
learned of repression from her Jewish grandmother. Her faith

in the state was always going to be circumspect. In the era of glasnost, my father was a voracious reader who wanted to learn the truth about Stalinism. But he never had that lived experience to make totalitarianism feel less like a difficult-to-pronounce word and more like a personal tragedy. It was one for Vera and my grandfather. But Alexander never shared his life story with his children.

Towards the end of my stay with my parents in Yekaterinburg, I help my father mend the greenhouse, which has been damaged by hail. 'Come back to Russia,' he tells me. 'The economy is growing, experienced strategists are in demand – you will find a job in a heartbeat. You won't have to pay a fortune for heating bills in London and you'll get to serve your motherland.' I'm standing on a stepladder, taping up holes on the roof. I continue the work and resist responding. I catch a glance of my father, his rigid figure a little stooped, his hair almost completely grey. He is still trim and in fairly rude health. But he will soon turn seventy, and he must feel my absence more acutely now.

But to me the idea of returning to Russia now is ghastly. It is like being invited to go back to Nazi Germany during the Second World War. I cannot entertain it at all. The current prosperity, boosted by the military economy, will come crashing down as most other industries are being neglected, the capital is no longer flowing into Russia and most of its young and brightest have fled the country. Clean streets and buzzing restaurants cannot entice me, and the spectre of the war will knock down these Potemkin villages soon enough. I love my friends here dearly, but this country is no longer my Russia. 'I cannot possibly stay,' I say to my father, disappointing him all over again.

Chapter 8

'I Couldn't Live There Any More'

I t is the last week of November. We are sitting on the terrace of a beachside restaurant in Valencia under an impossibly blue sky. We are here to celebrate Stella's birthday. She is another friend from Yekaterinburg I went to school with. Her daughter Ksenia is ordering seafood paella for the table in slightly accented, but already fluent, Spanish. Stella's thirteen-year-old son, Sergey, who now goes by Sergio, is complaining about the heat. His nine-year-old brother, Fedya ('They call me Fernando at school!'), is slouching over his games console. It's twenty-five degrees in the shade. Ordinarily, they'd be celebrating their mother's birthday amid the dark Russian winter with mugs of steaming hot chocolate, not bottles of Coca-Cola. The paella arrives in a huge pan, and we polish it off, scraping the burnt bits off the bottom. The boys ask if they can have ice-cream, and we oblige. We take lots of pictures and make the most of the afternoon, even going for a quick dip in the Mediterranean. It's the dream.

At dusk, we take a tram back to Stella's flat in one of Valencia's densely populated multinational neighbourhoods. There is a Sikh gurudwara opposite the tram stop, a Moroccan deli, a household supply store run by a Chinese family and a traditional bakery where I buy a bag of *polvorones de almendra,* Valencian almond treats. On weeknights, you can spot a fidgety youth selling drugs at the corner, 'but the police patrol the streets regularly, so we've never had any trouble,' says Stella. We climb the stairs of a visibly worse-for-wear apartment block, which reminds me of my late grandmother's building in our hometown. Here, instead of birches and poplars, the street is lined with orange trees.

The kids scatter to their rooms. The boys have online Spanish classes with a Russian tutor twice a week. Tomorrow it's back to school, where Fedya has at least some respite from the new language: one of his classmates is a Russian-speaking Ukrainian from Donetsk. Sergey isn't so lucky. His favourite lessons are English, maths and music, where he is learning to play the flute. Three months ago, when they first enrolled here, they didn't speak a word of Spanish beyond *'Hola'*. Their sister came to Valencia a year earlier to learn the language and prepare for the Spanish university entrance exams. She has now enrolled to study architecture. 'I was always at the top of the class in Russia,' she says, reminding me of her mother, 'but now I feel like a loser. I barely keep up. At home, I copy and paste lessons into a generative AI app on my iPad that dumbs things down for me.' She leaves to do her homework on the history of art and materials.

Stella and I return to the kitchen, where I pour wine into water glasses. 'Sorry,' says Stella, 'I haven't had the chance to buy wine glasses yet. Or a larger chopping board. Or a teapot.' She slaps her face, laughing. 'But at least we have inherited not one but two paella pans!'

The Antonov family moved into a cramped flat in Valencia from a spacious detached house with a garden and a basement gym in a high-end suburb of Yekaterinburg. Stella found the apartment with the help of a Russian-speaking broker and moved in with Ksenia. The boys joined them at the end of the summer. Stella's husband, Oleg, stayed behind in Russia. He is renovating the house, preparing to sell it in the new year before joining the rest of the family in Spain. As we sip our wine, the upstairs neighbours crank up the music. We can hear them singing along. The sound of fireworks bursts through the window. It's a world away from the tranquil gated development the family has left behind.

'We have been thinking about emigrating for a long time. Do you remember Putin winning the 2018 presidential elections? His first executive order was to call up army reservists for military training. Oleg's first career was in the army. We worried that Russia's intervention in Ukraine wouldn't end well.'

At that time, Stella was in charge of the Foreign Direct Investment and Innovation departments in the Ural Federal District, reporting to the Presidential Plenipotentiary in Yekaterinburg. Before Vladimir Putin came to power in 2000, Russia's regions enjoyed a certain degree of autonomy. They were in charge of their economic and investment policies and made their own budgetary decisions. In May 2000, Putin created six federal districts and appointed his own representatives to oversee regional decision-making. In theory, the additional layer was to support the implementation of constitutional laws and government policies in the region. In reality, it was a consolidation of his power. In 2009, the office of the Presidential Plenipotentiary moved into a new building on the bank of the River Iset. It is commonly referred to as 'Buckingham Palace' in Yekaterinburg, which gives one a fair idea of its architectural style and size. Stella had received the offer to join the team on the back of her academic work on foreign direct investment in the Urals. Ambitious and effective, she was soon in charge of the department. Stella's team met with powerful industrial magnates, who were keen to attract foreign capital to their metallurgical plants; she opened international economic forums in Yekaterinburg and met local lobbyists together with the Presidential Plenipotentiary in what was an increasingly autocratic business environment. She earned enough to build a house in a prestigious suburb, buy a new Toyota and take her family on holidays to Thailand in winter and Greece in the summer. At school reunions, Stella's former classmates openly envied her power and status. But soon after the 2018 presidential elections, she handed in her notice.

In September 2011, Russia's then president, Dmitry Medvedev, who was widely regarded as more progressive than his predecessor, announced that he was not going to seek re-election and would instead give the highest office in the country back to Vladimir Putin. The announcement came out as a bitter belch and prompted much discussion amid well-educated and democratically minded Russians. One such person was thirty-five-year-old Alexei Navalny, who wrote a popular blog exposing government corruption. He and other like-minded activists called on the usually politically apathetic Muscovites to show their opposition by voting against Putin's United Russia party in the December parliamentary elections. As a result, United Russia lost its two-thirds majority, though it still prevailed in the

Duma. Reports of widespread electoral fraud prompted Navalny to call on Muscovites to protest. Some 50,000 people showed up at Bolotnaya Square in Moscow in an unprecedented show of public opposition in Russia. The independent pollster Levada Centre estimated that only 35 per cent of Russians supported Putin at that time. Navalny was arrested and detained for a fortnight. He came out vowing to oppose the regime. People cheered. Many, like Stella, learned and remembered his name.

Barred from appearing on mainstream TV, Navalny launched his own YouTube channel. The first video, which revealed the secret riches of Dmitry Medvedev, including mansions, yachts and vineyards both in Russia and in Tuscany, clocked nearly fifty million views. Within a year, Navalny's Anti-Corruption Foundation released many such exposés of impudent embezzlement and corruption among government officials and others close to Putin. Stella and Oleg watched every one of them. When Putin extended his reign in 2018 to four more years, Stella decided she could not take it any more and left the office of the president's representative for academia.

Being back at university meant that Stella had more time for her children. She joined school committees, began picking up the kids and even started checking their homework. She wasn't being a helicopter parent – it's just that the school system had changed a lot since her own graduation in the middle of the 1990s.

In the early 2000s, the Unified State Exam was introduced in Russia to standardise school graduation and university entry exams. Previously, pupils had to take exams in May at the end of their final school year and sit exams at each university they were applying to a month later. The unified system, with compulsory mathematics and Russian and optional exams in other disciplines, was a much-needed educational reform. But, in time, high school education shifted from genuine learning towards memorisation and tutoring. While back in the 1990s we were encouraged to write essays and express our own opinions on *Crime and Punishment* or the poetry of the Silver Age, these days schoolchildren are being taught what to say about Raskolnikov in the exam to score a point, says Stella. When we were at school, we used to have six lessons of English a week; now the same school offers just three. This is because new subjects have been added to the school curriculum.

The Foundations of Secular Ethics has been taught to ten-year-old pupils in Russia since 2010. The first study block, 'Russia Is Our Motherland', focuses on the ethics and morals of being a patriot. The lessons outlined in the study guide include case studies from medieval Slavic tales where *bogatyrs* (strongmen) rescue princesses; lessons in modesty for 'gentlemen' and 'ladies'; traditional family values and the moral code of a 'defender of the Motherland'. The lessons teach children that while Russia is close and familiar, overseas is foreign and strange. Primary schoolchildren read a dated tale by the Soviet-Ukrainian writer Vasily Sukhomlinsky in which a peasant family would rather starve to death than travel across the sea for better pastures. As well as traditional Russian holidays such as New Year's Day and Women's Day (8 March), children are encouraged to honour the Day of the Security Officer (10 November) and the Day of the Defender of the Fatherland (23 February), which was more akin to a Father's Day during our childhood but has now reacquired a military connotation. The Day of National Unity, a new public holiday introduced in 2005, commemorates the liberation of Moscow from Polish invaders in the seventeenth century. It is meant to remind Russian people of the many adversities the country has faced over the centuries and of the selfless sacrifice necessary to maintain its safety and sovereignty. Like many other parents, Stella hired online tutors for her kids. They worked on their English twice a week after school.

In August 2020, at the end of school summer holidays in Russia, the Antonov family was following an extraordinary story. Navalny, whose Anti-Corruption Foundation Stella has been supporting with regular donations for many years, had collapsed on a flight returning to Moscow from Siberia. He stayed in a coma at a hospital in Omsk before being taken to Germany, where a consortium of experts diagnosed nerve-agent poisoning.

Stella remembers that fortnight well: 'Over the summer we were watching brave Belarusians protesting against the election stolen by Lukashenko, who had been in power since the mid-1990s. Navalny did a broadcast on his YouTube channel saying that Putin must be properly frightened by the revolutionary events in Belarus. And the next thing we know his life is hanging by a thread.'

In December that year, a team of European investigative journalists published a sensational report implicating the FSB in Navalny's poisoning. Posing as an official figure, Navalny himself called one of the FSB agents and questioned him about the details of the failed operation. The agent revealed that Novichok had been applied to Navalny's underwear in his hotel room in Tomsk. Incredibly, Navalny announced he was returning to Russia.

'We were waiting for him. His plane was full of journalists documenting his return. We followed his social media postings and every piece of news. We thought that now we would all unite and act! We wanted changes. *Our hearts demand changes! Our eyes demand changes!*' Stella is quoting the iconic lines from a

1990s song by the late Victor Tsoi. 'But at the same time, we knew well that Putin wouldn't leave him alone. They arrested him as soon as he returned.'

Navalny was arrested at passport control for violating the terms of his suspended sentence, relating to a 2014 embezzlement case he had always claimed was fabricated. He was put on trial in a makeshift courtroom set up at a police station in Khimki on the outskirts of Moscow. When a judge allowed him to speak, Navalny said, 'Don't be afraid. Take to the streets, not for me, but for yourselves, for your future.'

On Saturday, 23 January 2021, Stella and Oleg parked their car and made their way to the entrance of the Dynamo stadium in Yekaterinburg. It was bitterly cold. When the thermometer shows −30°C in Russia, people ordinarily spend as little time outdoors as possible. At most, they might nip out to get to work or pick up children from school, if the schools remain open. That day, as Stella and Oleg followed a crowd of people gathering to protest against Navalny's arrest, it was not just an act of bravery, but a feat of endurance. Stella recalls that she saw people of all ages, but the majority were in their forties and fifties. Most people wore disposable respiratory masks to keep warm. The meeting was supposed to take place near the stadium, but the crowd moved towards the embankment and kept walking along the frozen river. 'OMON', riot policemen in Russia, stood aside without interfering. A few of them were recording the march on camera. Some protesters carried placards demanding freedom for Navalny and for Russia; one man without a mask carried a stick with blue underwear attached to it, like a flag.

'The atmosphere was incredible. It was a real high. I felt I was among like-minded people and we were doing something important.' Afterwards, the regional authority reported that about 2,000 people had come out in Yekaterinburg, but non-government sources estimated that 10,000 protesters had braved the cold. The state media news didn't mention the protests at all, while social and Western media reported that people came out everywhere from Vladivostok in the Far East to Kaliningrad in the west. In Yakutsk, where the thermometer showed −52°C, several hundred gathered in the centre of town. More than 3,000 people were arrested that day across Russia. The following week, independent news websites in Yekaterinburg reported that some people had been subsequently arrested for taking part in an unsanctioned protest with the weekend video footage used to identify them.

'And then nothing. Nothing else happened except they sent Navalny to a strict-regime penal colony and kept adding years to his sentence. And we were given a message to put up and shut up.' Stella presses her lips together and sighs.

There were attempts to organise new protests the following weekends, but the authorities closed metro stations in the city centres of Moscow and St. Petersburg and used violence to disperse those who turned up. Some were hospitalised with severe injuries. In June 2021, Navalny's Anti-Corruption Foundation was declared an 'extremist organisation' for 'disseminating information that incited hatred and enmity against government officials' and 'destabilising Russia'. Its network of offices across Russia was shut down. All of its leaders and many other activists, who had by then faced multiple arrests and searches, fled to continue their work abroad. The authorities tightened the screw by detaining journalists and imposing fines on media outlets for spreading 'fake news' about dissent, but at the same time they allowed videos of their brutal crackdown to circulate on social media. The opposition leaders didn't stand a chance against such mass repression and fear. Three years later, in February 2024, Alexei Navalny died in an Arctic penal colony under mysterious circumstances. He was forty-seven years old. Over a thousand political prisoners remain in jail.

Sergey and Fedya burst into the kitchen asking about supper, and Stella rustles up something to eat. Ksenia takes a plate back to her room. She still has to prepare for her maths class. The boys eat in the living room and stay put, playing video games. It can't be easy to adjust to their new life here. As if reading my mind, Stella says, 'It's for them.'

She tells me about the first weeks after the war began. 'I was stunned. I couldn't stop crying. Then I found myself catching up with the new reality.' Stella and Oleg came to an agreed meeting place in Yekaterinburg to protest against the invasion, but before they even parked their car, they saw policemen shoving a man into a van. He shouted 'No to war!' before the door was slid shut. The entire area was cordoned off by the police. The rector of the university where Stella taught recorded a video stating that the only accepted opinion within the university would be the line of the official address by President Putin announcing the Special Military Operation. He invited all students and staff to draw the 'correct conclusion': to support the president and approve his course of action. He encouraged everyone to focus on education and concluded his speech with 'there can be no other position on this', making it clear that insubordination would not be tolerated. That same day everyone was invited to gather in front of the university entrance for the unveiling ceremony of a giant letter Z on the side of the building. Stella told her class she had planned an important seminar in the auditorium and, though it was their choice, they probably wouldn't want to miss it. They stayed. It was a tiny win against an academic establishment that had turned a blind eye to the one thing it was most supposed to hone: critical thinking.

'Critical thinking!' Stella is incensed again, remembering her colleagues in the staff room and their dogged determination to discuss anything except what was burning inside her. 'Some university! I too kept my mouth shut, well aware that anyone could snitch on me to the authorities and I'd get jailed. I have children. I couldn't do it.' At the end of that semester, she resigned.

'We have always talked openly to our children, so I told them that working and paying income tax to the state means that even if I am against the war, I am still supporting it indirectly,' says Stella. She also instructed her children not to express their views at school. She read about the director of a kindergarten who had threatened to report a mother to social services because her daughter had drawn a picture with a Ukrainian flag. 'I hated doing it. I didn't like to encourage that duplicity, but I had to.'

Meanwhile, school mums' WhatsApp groups were hyperactive. The school administration announced a collection for Russian soldiers on the front line. Mothers were busy comparing notes on what to donate: tea, chocolates, socks, painkillers. Someone suggested sanitary pads because they can be inserted into army boots as soft paddings. Stella says, 'I wanted to ask why our boys are there killing Ukrainian boys in the first place, but I didn't.' When she went to pick up Sergey after school, he said that they were told to write letters to the soldiers. The teacher made some helpful suggestions, like thanking our 'heroes' for 'defending the Motherland and keeping us safe'. Stella was shocked. It turned out that Sergey had refused. He had told the teacher he was a pacifist. Surprisingly, she let him off. He was the only person in his class who didn't conform.

In May 2022, at the end of the school year, Fedya reported that a demobilised soldier had come to speak to the children about patriotism. Stella was apoplectic. By that point, it was common knowledge that many front-line soldiers were mobilised convicts.

'I couldn't live there any more. I couldn't stay in a country where I cannot say what I think, where my children are taught nonsense at school and where there is no future for them. I want my children to be free. We had to leave.'

We sit still for a while. I ask Stella about freedom, a concept I don't often think about, living in London. Yet both Stella and I grew up with memories of Soviet citizens coming to the Manezhnaya Square in Moscow in August 1991 to protest against the *coup d'état* organised by the Communist Party hardliners and the head of the KGB, who sought to reverse Gorbachev's democratic reforms. Ordinary people encircled the tanks and refused to go back to terror, isolation and censorship. Stella was twelve and I was eleven. Freedom was something tangible then, but it soon got muddled with the more pressing matters of the early 1990s: the cost of living and economic survival, crime and lawlessness. It was entirely forgotten by the end of that decade. Stella remembers her mother breaking up her piggybank because the family needed the money to buy food. I recall my mother was robbed of her handbag and fur hat one winter evening when she was walking home from work.

Stella says, 'I've been thinking about freedom a lot. It's Navalny's slogan: "Russia Will Be Free!" It's the most important value for me: freedom to speak, to choose, to act. When we were growing up, we didn't pay attention to that, but now I want my children to live without the straitjacket of living in Russia.'

While we are discussing freedom in Valencia, the Russian parliament has approved a new bill tightening the existing restrictions on activities seen as promoting LGBT+ rights in Russia. The bill covers media, arts, advertising campaigns and any 'propaganda' of LGBT+ in public. The Kremlin spokesman described the LGBT+ movement as 'hybrid warfare against traditional Russian values'.

'And what gives them the right to decide this?' asks Stella.

A week later, Putin signs the bill into law, and the same day, the police raid a few gay clubs in Moscow. The Russian online movie database Kinopoisk has changed its rating of the rainbow-coloured *My Little Pony* series to 18+. Fear is never absurd.

'Will Russia be free?' I ask.

'Not within my lifetime,' says Stella.

'Not a chance?'

'You know what is the hardest thing to explain to a slave? That he is one.'

Chapter 9

The Accidentals[1]

K ira arrived at Vnukovo Airport in Moscow with plenty of time to spare. It was March 2022: she expected the departure area to be full of people like her, running away from Russia. Instead, the airport wasn't that busy. She strained to lift her luggage, which was unbelievably heavy – as absurd as it truly was: packing up her entire life into a suitcase, zipping it up and letting someone else carry it to a new destination she hadn't chosen or wished for. Now, with still two hours to spare before her departure, Kira slumped into a seat, hugging her carry-on bag and picking at the bleeding cold sore on her lip.

Up until three weeks ago, Kira's life had felt like a neat streak after a somewhat unstable childhood. Born in Shadrinsk, a small town in the Urals, her family first moved to Yekaterinburg and

---

1. In ornithology, an 'accidental' is a bird found outside of its normal geographic range, migration route or season.

then Moscow. Her parents divorced when Kira was fourteen, which taught her to be independent early on. She got an admin job in a construction company and studied IT after work. Her company was contracted by IKEA to build a new store in Moscow. Kira loved IKEA and always wanted to work there. At the end of the project, they offered her a job. She couldn't believe her luck. When asked if she spoke English, Kira replied that she'd learn it and then found herself a tutor that same day. Three months later, she signed up to a dating app hoping to find a native English speaker she could practise with. She matched with Dan, who worked for an Irish government agency in Moscow. He was born in Ireland, but his mother was originally from St. Petersburg. With Dan speaking fluent Russian, Kira didn't make much progress with the language, but they soon moved in together. Both in their mid-twenties, loving their jobs and everything that Moscow had to offer, Kira and Dan posted photos of themselves on social media with the Russian equivalent of #livingmybestlife. Nine months later, Putin invaded Ukraine.

Dan's employer repatriated him the following week. Before leaving, he said, 'Marry me. I'll look after you in Ireland.' Kira burst into tears. Even though they had been living together for months, Kira didn't feel like she knew Dan all that well. Besides, Kira wasn't some princess looking to be rescued. In any case, wasn't it all going to be over soon? Like all her friends, Kira was proudly 'apolitical'. But suddenly her bubble was burst. Dan helped her get a visa for Ireland, her understanding boss gave her leave and she bought a ticket to Dublin via Istanbul. It all happened on autopilot, fuelled by fear and panic. Once Dan left, Kira went to see her mother, who asked, 'Do you love him?' Kira was in floods again. She nodded yes between the sobs. 'Then you must go. There is no future here, Kira.'

Kira returned to Moscow three months later. She had to renew her Russian passport and apply for a new visa, this time as a spouse. She found that the city had changed. It wasn't anything tangible: in Moscow especially, the authorities strived to preserve the image of 'business as usual'. But it was as if the spectre of fear had crept deep into people's minds. On the metro, people seemed to be guarding their phone screens. Friends of Kira's went to great pains to talk about anything but war. There was a strain to their smiles. One family member didn't beat about the bush: 'Leaving, are you? Just don't tell me you don't like the people in power.' Kira shrugged in response. 'I got married.' Privately, she wondered why someone working three jobs to make ends meet would be happy with the Kremlin.

Shortly before Kira returned to Dublin in December 2022, an accidental fire destroyed a DIY store called OBI in the Khimki district of Moscow. It was part of the same megamall complex where Kira used to work. Videos of powerful explosions that set off car alarms in a nearby parking lot and ultimately burnt the building to the ground were all over the media. 'It felt like all of Russia was ablaze,' remembers Kira. 'Everything I worked for, everything I achieved – it was all gone. Putin wrecked my life!' That time she knew she would not be coming back, not until the war was over and there was regime change.

Kira's life as an immigrant didn't get off to a good start. Dan was transferred to London, but Kira had to wait for a UK visa for eight long months. Her in-laws were nice enough, but after the hive that is Moscow, living in a remote two-house Irish village surrounded by fields was a shock to the system. Dan visited when he could. Kira studied English and walked the dog. Her mother-in-law, who had left Russia thirty years ago, was a fan of Putin and his mission to 'clean up' Ukraine. Kira couldn't quite understand how someone who only occasionally came to Russia on holiday and was unfamiliar with the realities of ordinary Russian citizens could cast their vote for Putin the following year. After a very bleak period, her paperwork finally came through and Kira followed her husband to Britain.

I met Kira in London in 2024. She was one of many mostly young professionals who gathered at the Russian Embassy on Sunday, 17 March, at midday, for a protest masterminded by Alexei Navalny before his death. It was a clever plan: no one had any illusions about the outcome of the presidential election, but coming to the polling stations at the same time meant realising that, contrary to what the Kremlin wanted people to believe, there were plenty of Russians who opposed the regime. It was especially important, if somewhat unsafe, for people to see like-minded people in their own neighbourhoods in Russia. In London, people who joined the queue at midday ended up waiting for six to eight hours to cast their votes. It was the biggest social gathering of liberal Russians in London I've witnessed. Some people, like me, had only to jump on the Tube to get to Kensington. Others came from as far as Edinburgh, staying at a hotel in London overnight.

'I haven't even voted before,' confessed Kira. 'It felt like everything had been decided for me already, so I never bothered.' In London, Kira met some impressive people who drew live portraits as a hobby, debated nuclear physics and gave her advice on how to start looking for work. Kira found a part-time job assisting a digital entrepreneur, but she is aiming higher once she feels more confident about her English. Dan and Kira are still finding their feet in London, having to budget and learning how to cook now that takeaway and eating out have become a luxury, but London is a vibrant new world they are both keen to explore.

'At first I was nervous to say I was Russian,' says Kira. 'But very quickly I realised that while some people make sympathetic noises, most simply don't care. Everyone has their own problems, here and in Ireland. As long as you behave like a decent human being, you're welcome.'

According to a study by the independent Russian newspaper *The Bell*, some 650,000 people who left Russia since the start of the full-scale invasion of Ukraine are still abroad. Journalists studied data from some seventy countries and found that Georgia, Armenia, Kazakhstan and Israel had together taken in nearly 350,000 migrants, mostly bright young professionals able to work remotely. Nearly 50,000 Russians chose the US and 15,500 came to the UK. While the total number may be even higher in the absence of data from such countries as Thailand and Portugal, popular with Russian nomads, it already represents the largest exodus from Russia in the last twenty years. (Previously, c. 1.5 to 3 million Russians left their homes in 1918–22 and some 1.6 million are estimated to have left for the West during the 1990s.) This explains the Kremlin's policies to exempt IT workers from military duty and extend state support to parents, announced in February 2024. A mother is rewarded with 630,400 rubles (c. £5,300) for the birth of her first child and 883,000 rubles (c. £7,400) for the birth of her second and subsequent children. The Russian government is well aware of the skilled-labour shortages and the country's demographic problems.

While some Russians who rushed for the border in September 2022 following the government's partial mobilisation announcement returned shortly thereafter, most people who left have not come back. What is their experience abroad? And what is the effect of their migration on host countries?

Georgia, a small neighbour of Russia with a population of 3.7 million, famous for its beautiful Caucasus Mountains, access to the Black Sea, excellent cuisine and ancient vineyards, was the first port of call for many people fleeing Russia. This is because Russian citizens could stay in Georgia visa-free for a year and reset the clock by hopping over the border to Armenia for a day. Russia also shares a land border with Georgia, so many travelled there by car. By the end of 2022, about 110,000 Russians had moved to the country. Inevitably, some arrived there having never been abroad before or given much thought to the simmering geopolitical tensions between the countries. Anecdotally, some Russians were not even aware of the fact that since 2008 Russian military forces have been stationed in Abkhazia and South Ossetia, the would-be separatist regions Georgia still regards as part of its sovereign territory. Having arrived, guests were surprised to learn that Georgians of the same age were often fluent in English or German but didn't speak Russian. Soon after the influx, some parts of Tbilisi and Batumi on the Black Sea became overwhelmed with Russians. Between 2022 and 2023, some 200 new Russian bars and restaurants were opened and 26,000 new companies were registered. The Russian language became a common sound on the streets, which must have felt uncomfortable to most citizens of this proudly independent state. And prices nearly doubled in the rental market, causing resentment. Anti-Russian graffiti and occasional bar fights were perhaps unavoidable and the general distrust and animosity also predictable. The Russian Empire and its successor, the Soviet Union, had control over the Caucasus from the middle of the nineteenth century. Very little has been done in Russia since the break-up of the Soviet Union in 1991 to change Russian people's possessive attitude towards their neighbours.

In a September–October 2023 public opinion poll, 73 per cent of Georgians said that Russian citizens should no longer be allowed visa-free entry, or to register a business or buy property in Georgia. Not feeling welcomed, more than 30,000 Russians were reported to have left Georgia in 2023, leaving 73,562, reported *The Bell*. In May 2024, despite mass protests in Tbilisi, the Georgian government adopted a 'Law on Transparency of Foreign Influence', making media organisations and NGOs with more than 20 per cent funding from abroad subject to detailed financial disclosures, increased state scrutiny and potential restrictions. It was dubbed 'the Russia law' because of the virtually identical law that exists in Russia. It is fair to assume that this development did not improve the attitudes of ordinary Georgians towards Russian migrants, who, as a result, will probably move on to new pastures. One such couple left Georgia for Serbia and gave an interview to *Radio Free Europe*. Their decision to relocate was due to frequent water and electricity shortages in Tbilisi, expensive but unreliable internet and the 'low-grade hostility that they felt from Georgians'. The last straw was getting into a taxi with their parents who were visiting from Russia. Inside the driver had a sign in English: 'Russians go home.' Fortunately, their parents did not speak English, but that incident made up their minds. The couple explained that while some apprehension on the locals' part is understandable, 'no one wants to have to prove every day that they are "good Russians"'.

Some 110,000 Russians settled in neighbouring Armenia, a country with a population of 2.78 million. Like Georgia, it offers a visa-free regime, and there are frequent flights to Yerevan from several cities in Russia. The warm attitude towards Russians stems from Russia being Armenia's ally in the conflict over Nagorno-Karabakh, a disputed mountainous region situated between Armenia and Azerbaijan. Even the military takeover of Nagorno-Karabakh by Azerbaijan in September 2023, ostensibly condoned by Russia, has not led to resentment. Arayik, a travel guide who once took me on a tour of ancient churches and monasteries of Armenia and up Aragats, its tallest mountain, says that Armenians do not equate ordinary Russians with the people in the Kremlin: 'We understand that some people have had enough and came to Armenia for refuge. Most Russians who arrived here treat locals with respect, their children are at school with our children and they are good neighbours. Some are even learning Armenian. There are exceptions, but those are exceptions.'

Most Russian migrants are young, educated, economically independent and work in the IT sector, which is also strong in Armenia, with well-developed broadband infrastructure in the capital Yerevan and Gyumri, the second biggest city. Several Russian companies, such as Miro and Yandex, have opened offices in Armenia, also creating jobs for Armenian IT specialists. The influx of migrants has caused some inflation, but Armenia's two-digit economic growth, boosted not only by domestic consumption but also by buoyant exports fuelled by goods bypassing the economic sanctions on Russia, has had a net positive development on the country's economy. When I ask Arayik whether his travel business has benefited from new Russian clients, he shakes his head: 'I don't think IT geeks like hiking very much.' Previously, he advertised his services exclusively in Russia, but he fears that the latest Kremlin rhetoric condemning Armenia for becoming friendly with the West is putting people who watch Russian TV off from travelling to the country. 'Politics.' He shrugs.

Another refuge for Russian migrants is Kazakhstan. Nearly one million Russians, mostly men, crossed the border into

Kazakhstan in September 2022 after the announcement of partial mobilisation. Many returned home a month later, but those who stayed – around 80,000 – found it relatively easy to settle. Russian is widely spoken in Kazakhstan, and about 15 per cent of the population of nearly 20 million is ethnically Russian. According to Kazakh media, many doctors, teachers, IT specialists, farm and service workers found jobs there on arrival. Locals are much more tolerant to Russian migrants than in Georgia, but in many ways Kazakhstan is a more conservative country. Its government controls political activism, and its society is largely patriarchal and illiberal concerning sexual identity. Though homosexuality is decriminalised, gay marriage and civil partnership are illegal. This chimes well with the government position in Russia. On the other hand, young migrants coming to Kazakhstan from Russia tend to be much more liberal. I speak to a couple who came to Almaty from Yekaterinburg in September 2022 and left for Thailand about a year later. Polina explains that both she and her husband are self-employed and able to work from anywhere in the world, provided they have decent broadband access. They found a nice flat and travelled around at weekends, exploring the country, but it wasn't a place they thought of as home. 'I found the local society pretty insular and conservative,' says Polina. 'In Yekaterinburg, I lived in a liberal bubble, surrounded by successful female entrepreneurs and outspoken intellectuals. The traditional gender roles and regressive attitudes towards women and minorities in Kazakhstan were too much of a shock. It's hard to explain, but out on the street I felt invisible as a woman. I didn't like that one bit.'

Many Russian migrants see Georgia, Armenia and Kazakhstan as a temporary base. They call themselves *relokanty*, 'relocated'. The words 'exile' or even 'immigration' are not in their vocabulary. They are not planning to return to Russia in the near future, but they are exploring other options. Thailand and Vietnam are popular in the winter months, and some even travel as far as Central and South America, where many countries, including Argentina, Chile, Costa Rica and Honduras, allow Russians to enter without a visa for a short-term stay. Young and savvy, they are not very different from digital nomads brought up in the West.

I met one former Russian nomad, Anton, in the embassy queue in March 2024 as well, and we arranged to meet for a coffee the following week. A product developer from Moscow who cut his teeth at leading tech companies in Russia, Anton had been working remotely from Thailand during the winter months long before the pandemic. In 2019, he was invited to come to London to help build a start-up founded by a Russian entrepreneur. Two years later, Anton was headhunted by a prominent British tech business and joined as a lead product developer. Now he and a couple of co-founders are building their own venture. I told him I used to work in venture capital and said I'd have a look at his business plan.

Anton, who is in his mid-thirties, has the athletic build of someone who starts his day with meditation, bulletproof coffee and calisthenics. He gives the impression of being a well-rounded person with just the right blend of confidence and humility you want to see in an entrepreneur. He makes me laugh as he tells me about getting used to the different way of working here in the UK: there's less 'stick' and swearing than you'd encounter in a fast-growing business in Moscow. Anton surprised himself during the two years he worked for the British tech company by getting on board with conversations about burnout, mental health and company culture. 'It turns out, bosses here can get the best out of people without shouting at them,' he says with a smile. A Russian with a sense of humour, I observe.

His business presentation is slick. Investing in early-stage start-ups is not particularly scientific as there are few data points you can rely on at first. The founders' background plays a key role. Anton's slides show that he and his co-founders have decades of relevant experience in building and scaling complicated tech businesses in London and Tallinn. There is no reference to Russian Yandex or Tinkoff, where I know Anton had worked. I look closer at the biography of the Chief Technology Officer. His name is Anthony Smith. His photo bears an uncanny resemblance to the person sitting opposite me.

'Would *you* put your Russian name on a pitch deck to raise money?' he asks.

I hate to admit it, but he has a point. Venture capitalists get hundreds of pitches that they scan through quickly. A Russian founder could well be perceived as a red flag bound to be raised by an investment committee. No one would get blamed for saying no to a pitch from a Russian. There are plenty of other opportunities without opening that potential can of worms.

'Won't they find out anyway when they meet you?'

'Yes, we got some feedback already. They cited reservations about our ability to build a cohesive team and our communication skills. It must be my accent.'

Anton doesn't appear discouraged, explaining that they are making progress without external funding and should be in a stronger position later when they have more to show for themselves.

'Why jump ship in the first place? An entrepreneurial itch to scratch?'

Anton is silent. 'Something like that,' he says eventually.

Anton had led product development at the British start-up for nearly two years. His manager couldn't have been happier with him. Thanks to Anton and his team, the business had released the new product features they'd been promising to investors since the previous funding round. Then, one day in spring 2022, Anton opened the door to a meeting room, expecting to see his boss. Instead, he was greeted by two stony-faced HR employees.

'I signed, like, twenty NDAs.' Anton won't talk about what happened, but his face betrays unfair dismissal.

'Did you get legal advice?'

'I sure did.'

I don't press him further. It's one side of the story, and I don't want to get him into trouble. Anton landed on his feet and does freelance work for companies in Tel Aviv, Toronto and Dubai. He also tells me about his Russian friend in London who received a notice from his landlord demanding he move out. It was March 2022. The landlord explained it was nothing personal, just a precaution in case his Russian tenant lost his job or had his bank account frozen. Anton's friend didn't want a confrontation. He sublet a room from a Russian buddy with a British passport instead.

Anton tells me that his Telegram channels are full of stories like that.

The last week of November is a strange month to be travelling to Helsinki. The city is cold and dark and not yet dressed up for Christmas. And yet this is the time the Finnish capital transforms into a buzzing networking hub of tech entrepreneurs and venture capitalists here for Slush. It's the largest gathering in the global start-up scene, featuring talks and workshops, pitching

events, media exposure and informal shoulder-rubbing opportunities, culminating in Slush 100 – 'the most coveted start-up
competition in the world'. The winner, judged by a panel of top
venture capitalists, receives €1 million of equity funding. It's
nearly too good to be true.

In November 2022, the winner was Immigram, a business that
helps IT specialists and other tech talent relocate to the UK, nav-
igating the Global Talent visa-application process. The start-up
launched in 2019 and prospered during the pandemic, impressing
the judges with its traction. Immigram founders were invited on
stage and handed a giant cheque, signed by investment companies like Accel, General Catalyst, Lightspeed Venture Partners,
NEA and Northzone. But less than twenty-four hours later the
dream turned into a nightmare. Slush revoked Immigram's win
and issued a muddled statement of apology.

As soon as the winners were announced, a Ukrainian-born
participant had taken to social media calling Slush 'tone-deaf'.
Many echoed him. The winners, Anastasia Mirolyubova and
Mikhail Sharonov, were born in Russia and still hold Russian
passports despite residing abroad. Mirolyubova has lived in the
UK since 2016, which is where Immigram was registered as a business. The majority of Immigram's early adopters were Indians,
but since the full-scale invasion of Ukraine, many Russian IT
specialists have chosen Immigram to help with their UK paperwork. Mirolyubova (her surname translates from Russian
as 'peace-loving') and Sharonov spoke out against the war.
The founders' background and Immigram's traction in Russia
should have been discovered during due diligence – after all, the
competition was open for months ahead of the conference. No
venture fund would commit its capital without doing some basic
background work on a potential investment opportunity.

Social media amplified the understandable outrage of the
Ukrainian participant and his allies, and Mirolyubova issued
her own statement in response to the furore, getting ahead of
the organisers: 'Immigram opts out of the Slush competition. We
will continue supporting Ukraine and building a company for
millions of talented people who want to move internationally.'
Without clear guidance from Slush, the start-up community
jumped to their own conclusions, posting about the founders'
Russian passports and the company's Russian and Belarusian
backers and their activities. Helping people leave Russia was
cited as particularly deplorable. As so often happens during a
social media frenzy, both Mirolyubova and Sharonov received
death threats.

Now, nearly two years later, neither of the founders wanted to
talk about their experience, but they indicated that both the war
and the aftermath of what happened at Slush had taken their toll.
Immigram, though, has been doing well, continuing to help IT
specialists from all over the world relocate to the UK. And a 2023
report by The Entrepreneurs Network stated that 39 per cent of
the UK's fastest-growing start-ups have at least one immigrant
co-founder. In the US, 43 per cent of companies in the 2017
Fortune 500 and 52 per cent of its top twenty-five were founded
or co-founded by an immigrant or the child of an immigrant,
famously including Google's Moscow-born Sergey Brin.

Though Immigram certainly suffered a backlash, my further
enquiries into Western 'Russophobia' proved fruitless. No one I
spoke to had been discriminated against, or at least not to their
knowledge. While in Russia, I remember talking to a woman
whose son got a job in Prague and moved there with his family.
'They have nice neighbours, and no one bothers them on the
street,' she said. 'I was so worried about them, because we are

told everyone in the West hates Russians.' Ultimately, the term 'Russophobia' has been popularised by the Kremlin to convince the population that Putin is retaliating in response to a deep anti-Russian sentiment sown by Britain and the US. Persecution of Russian and Russian-speaking people is one of Putin's justifications for invading Ukraine. By condemning 'Russophobia', the Kremlin equates opposition to its policies with anti-Russian prejudice, melding the state and its people. But as far as Western governments are concerned, Putin's tactics have not been mirrored here. On 14 March 2023, Fergus Eckersley, UK political coordinator at the UN, made a statement on Russophobia, addressing the Security Council:

Colleagues, Russophobia is one of the ever-growing list of excuses that Russia has come up with to justify its war in Ukraine. The fact that they are inventing so many of these is itself a good indication that they know none of them stands up to full scrutiny. Let me be clear, on behalf of the UK, and let me say it in Russian:

Мы не русофобы. Наоборот, у нас есть исторические отношения между нашими странами. Мы вместе сражались в двух мировых войнах. Мы глубоко уважаем богатое культурное наследие России. Я сам семь лет изучал русский язык, его историю и замечательную литературу.[2]

We do not want Russia to fail as a state, as the Russian

---

2. We do not suffer from Russophobia. We have a long history between our two countries. We fought together in two world wars. Across our country people respect and admire Russia's rich cultural heritage. I myself spent seven years studying Russia's language, its history and its remarkable literature.

delegation sometimes claims. Quite the opposite, in fact. We want Russia to be a stable and prosperous nation – just one that does not invade and try to annex its neighbours.

The enduring love for Russia's cultural heritage is ubiquitous. London theatres keep staging Chekhov's plays; the Proms or the Royal Opera House season would be impossible to imagine without Tchaikovsky, Shostakovich, Rachmaninov, Prokofiev or Stravinsky. Russian immigrants, wary about public attitudes at the beginning of the full-scale invasion of Ukraine, have largely enjoyed sympathy and support from their friends and colleagues in the West. As for the hatred towards newly migrated Russians, it only comes from people back home. I spoke to a couple in their sixties who had relocated to Tel Aviv in November 2022. They had already been learning Hebrew and preparing to move to Israel for some years for their retirement. The war was the impetus that sped things up. Over Zoom, they told me about getting used to the heat, their morning walks by the sea, the cultural events and community initiatives that keep them busy. I asked them about their friends and family in Russia.

'What do they say about your move?'

'Most are happy for us. But some have called us "rats" and "traitors" leaving Russia for "a warmer climate" when "the Motherland needs everyone's unwavering support".'

The resigned sadness in their eyes was heartbreaking.

Chapter 10

Cancel Putin not Pushkin

The Royal Albert Hall is full. The musicians of the BBC Philharmonic Orchestra have taken their seats. At last, the conductor John Storgårds walks to the podium to general applause. The sense of anticipation is interrupted only by a few coughs and some last-minute shuffles. Storgårds looks up, raises his hands and at once the silence is pierced by a shrill and unsettling cacophony of sounds which soon settles into an urgent march. It can only be Shostakovich's Fourth. From the comfort of my cushioned seat at the most beautiful music venue in London, I'm transported to the Leningrad of early 1936, where twenty-nine-year-old Dmitry Shostakovich is working on his new symphony. In January that year, the general secretary of the Communist Party of the Soviet Union, Joseph Stalin, had attended a performance of Shostakovich's *Lady Macbeth of Mtsensk*, an opera that had enjoyed considerable success since its premiere in 1934, not only in the Soviet Union, but also in New

York, London, Stockholm and Zürich. Stalin left before the end. Two days later a review with an ominous title, 'Muddle Instead of Music', appeared in *Pravda*. It was unsigned. Some rumoured it was penned by Stalin himself, but it was in fact written by an opportunistic journalist, David Zaslavsky, who got the gist of the despot's views right. The opera unleashed a torrent of criticism in the press and left Shostakovich fearing for his life. He even kept a suitcase in his apartment, packed with warm clothes and sturdy boots in case they came to arrest him.

British conductor Mark Wigglesworth writes about how, in 1936, the composer's life turned upside down: 'To know him was dangerous; to associate with him was suicidal.' Shostakovich's Fourth symphony was due to premiere in December in Leningrad. However, the composer decided to withdraw it from the repertoire, claiming that the finale needed rewriting. More likely, fearing for himself and the safety of the Leningrad Philharmonic Orchestra, Shostakovich had bowed to public pressure. The symphony was finally performed in December 1961, during the Khrushchev Thaw, nine years after Stalin's death and nearly three decades after it was written.

In an interview with the BBC, John Storgårds calls the Fourth Symphony Shostakovich's 'most spectacular and personal'. Music scholars agree that, far from exercising restraint after the takedown of his earlier opera, Shostakovich remained true to his original ideas, completing it in a spirit of uncompromising defiance. Russian culture expert Rosamund Bartlett confirms that the modernist language of the Fourth is very different from Shostakovich's later symphonies, which sound more 'conformist'. It is his grandest work, composed for an orchestra of more than 120.

It is also deeply human. Wigglesworth recalls the words of

Nadezhda Mandelstam, wife of the poet Osip Mandelstam, who was arrested for his satirical poem about the regime and Stalin personally and exiled in 1934. He died in Gulag. His poem, which compared Stalin's moustache to that of a cockroach, wasn't published but was recited to a small group of friends and then reported to the authorities. Osip himself described the 1930s as the time when 'we live, but we can't feel the land under our feet'. His wife's memoir, *Hope Against Hope*, gives a harrowing eyewitness account of the terror during Stalin's purges. Wigglesworth quotes:

> An existence like this leaves a mark. We all become slightly unbalanced mentally, not ill, but not normal either: suspicious, mendacious, confused and inhibited in our speech, at the same time putting on a show of adolescent optimism. If you live in a state of constant panic, you begin to have a special awareness of each minute, of each second. Time drags on, acquiring weight and pressing down on the breast, like lead.

Perhaps this is what Shostakovich sought to convey through his music. Nearly a century later, the Fourth resonates like never before.

The BBC Philharmonic received a generous ovation at the Royal Albert Hall. So did other orchestras performing Tchaikovsky, Rachmaninov, Stravinsky, Mussorgsky, Prokofiev and more Shostakovich during the 2024 Proms season. The audience welcomed many Russian-born soloists and conductors, including Kirill Petrenko, who succeeded Sir Simon Rattle to lead the Berlin Philharmonic; music director of the Royal Philharmonic Orchestra, Vasily Petrenko (unrelated to Kirill); pianist Denis Kozhukhin; soprano Aida Garifullina;

and Yekaterinburg-born cellist Anastasia Kobekina. They have all been applauded for their performances. I can imagine how deeply important that must have been for them.

One prominent Russian conductor has been absent though – and for a very good reason. Valery Gergiev, director of the Mariinsky Theatre in St. Petersburg, has been friends with Vladimir Putin since the early 1990s, when the conductor was gaining prominence and a post-KGB Putin worked in St. Petersburg's city administration. Over the last decade, Gergiev has become one of the most vocal supporters of Putin's regime among the Russian cultural elite, conducting propaganda concerts at Palmyra's Roman Theatre to an audience of Russian soldiers, who had supported Syrian government forces against Islamic State militants, endorsing the annexation of Crimea and even posing for photos with Russian army generals. Despite that, Gergiev's career in the West had continued to flourish. He was the principal conductor of the London Symphony Orchestra from 2007 to 2015 before moving on to the Munich Philharmonic. He led prominent music festivals and performed at the Met.

On 23 February 2022, Gergiev conducted Tchaikovsky's *Queen of Spades* at La Scala in Milan. The following day Russia invaded Ukraine. The mayor of Milan made a statement: the show wouldn't go on unless Gergiev denounced the war and his master. Other cities, including Munich and Rotterdam, echoed the call. Gergiev said nothing. His standing engagements in the West were cancelled. In a way, the guardians of Western art and culture acted more decisively than their counterparts in the Reichstag, Palazzo Chigi or the White House.

I shall not miss Gergiev, but I'm grateful for Tchaikovsky. In the last few years, Russian classical music has become increasingly important to me. This opulent cultural heritage has endured ineffective monarchs, the Bolshevik Revolution, the capricious whims of the Red Tsar, long years of stagnation and the dire times at the end of the last century as the Soviet Union inevitably ripped at the seams. It will also outlive this shameful period of Russian history. Autocracies fall. Kleptocrats will eventually run out of rope. But Rachmaninov's Piano Concerto No. 2, Tchaikovsky's *Swan Lake*, Prokofiev's *Romeo and Juliet*, Stravinsky's *The Rite of Spring* and Mussorgsky's *Pictures at an Exhibition* will keep enchanting and healing souls around the world for ever.

Not everyone agrees. In July 2024, Ukrainian authorities in Odessa decided to rename eighty-four streets of the Ukrainian port city to break their association with the Soviet past and strengthen national identity. 'Tchaikovsky Lane will become Theatre Lane, Pushkin Street will become Italian Street, Babel Street will become Dmytro Ivanov Street, Ilf and Petrov Street will become the Glodan Family Street, Bunin Street will become Nina Strokata Street', they announced, and so on. Besides the common Russian-language heritage (Russian is widely spoken in Odessa), all of them had lived in Odessa and written about it. Ilya Ilf and Yevgeny Petrov, the remarkable writing duo behind the classic satirical novels *The Twelve Chairs* (1928) and *The Golden Calf* (1931), were Odessan natives. Pushkin wrote about Odessa in his most famous novel in verse, *Yevgeny Onegin*, praising the city's vibrancy and European attitudes. Nobel-Prize winning author Ivan Bunin loved Odessa and stayed there before leaving Russia for France after the Bolshevik Revolution. Isaac Babel, the acclaimed Jewish short story writer, was born in Odessa and set many of his stories there. In my favourite Babel story, 'My First Goose', a young graduate joins the Cossack army during the Polish–Soviet War (1919–21). In an effort to fit in, he slaughters a poor woman's goose and orders her to cook it, impressing his comrades. However, at night, he is tormented by his act of violence and cannot sleep. Babel, who worked as a war correspondent and later wrote stories based on his experiences, was arrested by the NKVD (the predecessor to the KGB) on fabricated charges of terrorism and espionage and shot in 1940 at the age of forty-five.

In his book *The Language of War*, Ukrainian author Oleksandr Mykhed writes that 'Russian culture is an integral part of a repressive imperial machine'. He elaborates that his hatred isn't directed exclusively towards Putin and his strong-men, but extends to all Russian people and the very idea of 'Russianness'. In an interview with the *Financial Times*, Mykhed says he is 'infuriated by the insouciant tendency in the West to link Ukrainian writers with exiled Russians, as if they have some kind of pan-Slavic kinship, and also by the quest to explore the "Russian soul".' To him, there is no such thing as the 'Russian soul': 'There is just void in it.' Mykhed likes the idea of erasing Russian names from Ukrainian streets and tearing down statues of Pushkin, which he regards as emblems of the Russian hegem-ony. 'I think that Russia is using their culture as an instrument of hybrid warfare.' When the *Financial Times* photographer positioned him in front of birch trees for a portrait – purely by chance – Mykhed moved away to avoid the 'classic Russian framing'. He calls for the West to stop romanticising Russian culture, pull out its roots and focus on the barbaric atrocities being committed by Russia in Ukraine.

I read Mykhed's words at the same time the National Theatre of Latvia terminated a contract for the performance of the Russian-language play *Notes of a Madman*, about two people lost in space and time, struggling to find their purpose in difficult circumstances. Chulpan Khamatova, who had publicly denounced the Kremlin and the war and left Russia for Latvia in February 2022, had been cast as the lead. Fortunately, the production found a different venue for the show.

How do I feel about this dislike of all things Russian? Can I understand where this hatred is coming from? Yes, I can. The Russians effectively annexed Latvia in 1939 as part of the Molotov–Ribbentrop Pact between Nazi Germany and the Soviet Union, invading and occupying the country along with Lithuania and Estonia in June 1940. In January 1991, Mikhail Gorbachev sent tanks into Latvia and Lithuania to halt their democratic uprisings. Fourteen civilian protesters were killed in Lithuania. I don't have the heart to list all the atrocities committed by the Russian forces in Ukraine since 2014, but if I were from a country invaded by Russia, I'd hate me too.

But as a Russian, I have a different perspective. It wasn't Pushkin who raped and looted in Bucha; it wasn't Tchaikovsky who carpet-bombed Mariupol. The Russian language is how in *Life and Fate* Vasily Grossman told the world about Stalin's purges, Hitler's gas chambers and the brutalities of the Second World War. It helped Solzhenitsyn endure the Gulag. It's the language of the Belarusian Nobel-Prize laureate Svetlana Alexievich, who recorded ordinary people's experiences post Chernobyl, during the Soviet war in Afghanistan and the lawlessness of the 1990s. Russian culture embodies values antithetical to the inhumanity and hollowness of Putin's regime and will one day help Russia prevail over evil.

In the meantime, calls to cancel Russian culture only play into Putin's hands. The Kremlin propaganda machine picks up those voices and amplifies them to grotesque proportions, feeding into its own narrative about Russia being attacked by enemies across the Western world. In parallel, though, the Russian authorities are waging their own war on contemporary arts.

Since 2022, Russian authorities have labelled many Russian singers, artists and writers as 'foreign agents', including singers Boris Grebenshchikov, Zemfira and Yekaterinburg-born Monetochka; lead singers from The Time Machine and Little Big; rappers Face and Oxxxymiron; film director Alexander Rodnyansky; actor Artur Smolyaninov; TV personality Tatiana Lazareva; Russia's most prolific author, Grigory Chkhartishvili, who writes under the pen name Boris Akunin; International Booker Prize nominee Ludmila Ulitskaya; classical pianist Evgeny Kissin; and many others.

The Kremlin did not stop there. In May 2023, the playwright Svetlana Petriychuk and theatre director Yevgenia Berkovich were arrested on charges of 'justification of terrorism' for their play *Finist Yasny Sokol* ('Finist, the Fine Falcon', named after a brilliant strongman from Russian folk tales). The play tells the story of Russian women who meet members of ISIS online and attempt to reach Syria to marry them. It is based on real criminal cases of women put on trial in Russia for assisting terrorism. In 2021 and 2022, the play received multiple nominations and prestigious awards in Russia. Nevertheless, in July 2024, Petriychuk and Berkovich were both sentenced to six years in penal colonies.

Most people in Russia who get their information from the mainstream media know little about dissident rappers or the jailed theatre director, who is a mother to two adopted children. State TV channels broadcast pop concerts with headliners waving Russian flags between songs and leading the crowd in chants of 'Rossiya! Rossiya!' Shaman, the Kremlin's poster boy, released the song 'I am Russian' shortly after the full-scale invasion of Ukraine. Its many videos on YouTube have millions of views. Filip Kirkorov, Dima Bilan, Valeria, Oleg Gazmanov, Masha Rasputina, Larisa Dolina, Lyube and many others endorsed Putin during the 2024 presidential elections, performing in occupied territories in Ukraine and making public statements supporting the invasion. Yet, like in the general population at large, many others have remained silent.

Perhaps most depressingly, some of the genuinely talented Russian artists have become the staunchest supporters of the regime. Nikita Mikhalkov is a Russian filmmaker and actor, whose 1994 film *Burnt by the Sun* won the Grand Prix at Cannes and an Academy Award for the Best Foreign Language Film. In the film, set in the late 1930s, a senior Red Army officer (played by Mikhalkov) who has distinguished himself in the Civil War and believes himself to be well regarded by Stalin, is arrested on fabricated charges and then shot. I loved that film. There have not been enough books, films, plays or educational programmes in Russia to help us process the Stalinist times as a nation. Instead, new statues and portraits of the Red Tsar have begun to be erected again all over Russia under Putin's leadership. In 2021, Russia's Supreme Court ordered the closure of Memorial International, a human rights group founded in the 1980s that built a database of the victims of Soviet repression and has been helping relatives trace missing people. The state prosecutor portrayed the organisation as a geopolitical weapon used by foreign governments to deprive modern Russians from taking pride in the achievements of the Soviet Union. As for Mikhalkov, he got involved in politics by becoming the greatest sycophant on state TV. A self-described monarchist, in 2007 he signed an open letter asking Putin to stay in the office at the end of his second term. In 2022, he was finally sanctioned by the EU for his support for the invasion of Ukraine.

When I was in Russia, I saw what happens to contemporary culture when it dwells between a rock and a hard place. Yekaterinburg has many theatres, yet, as I've seen for myself, their repertoires are limited to uncontroversial classic plays and light comedies. It was such a contrast to the vibrant theatre scene I'm used to in London. When I asked my friends about any underground theatre, art or music responding to the tightening of the authoritarian regime, they only shook their heads.

What about the other Russia, dispersed all over the world and likely to remain so for some time? Is there hope that Russian culture can flourish in exile?

A queue of tourists is waiting to enter the Rijksmuseum to see paintings by some of the world's masters. I arrive in Amsterdam with a different agenda. I follow the canal and head to De Balie, a contemporary arts centre, which is hosting an exhibition, *Artists Against the Kremlin*, organised by a Dutch media outlet, the *Moscow Times* and the Berlin-based gallery and artist community All Rights Reversed. They have put together a collection of more than a hundred works by Russian-speaking artists from Belarus, Russia and Ukraine, united by their anti-war stance. Many of the participating artists live in exile. Some sign their works using pseudonyms.

Many works have been inspired by the war itself. *РОЖАЙ!* (*Breed!*) by K. Hell is a sign made out of pieces of broken toy soldiers. There is a picture of a Soviet pioneer by Masha Bolotina: he is saluting with one hand while his other holds a handgun to his temple. A banner above him says 'BE READY!', an oath I remember swearing myself in 1988, promising to be ready to serve my Motherland. Two works by olo.olooloolo display *kokoshniks*, traditional Russian headdresses worn by married women until the nineteenth century. Here one is made of cartridges with a centrepiece in the shape of a cross one might see above a grave. Another *kokoshnik* is decorated with prison tattoos, alluding to the many Russian convicts who have been pardoned in exchange for signing up to fight in the war with Ukraine. Antik Danov, a Ukrainian artist working under a pseudonym, designed a series of outdoor advertising posters and installed them in public places in Crimea in 2023 before photographing them. The posters say: 'I pretend that I cannot change anything', 'I pretend there is no war' and 'I pretend that this doesn't concern me'. In the same vein, Mikhail Ray used an image of a man's face with his eyes and mouth sewn shut in the shape of the letter 'Z'. Perhaps the most striking work is a simple white canvas by Nadya Raplya on which is written, 'It's too fucking late to draw.'

Other works paint a more general picture of contemporary Russia. There is a wall switch with two positions: 'TV' and 'Brain'. Berlin-based artisterror called this piece *Easy Choice*. Pomidor art group has created an embroidered textile displaying the phrase 'I just wanna talk about it', a comment on the overwhelming majority of people in Russia who want to do the exact opposite. *Coat of Arms of Putin's Russia*, a 2011 print by Manifestophilus, shows the logo of the federal state TV channel '1' in the centre, surrounded by handcuffs, FSB shoulder marks, radioactive poison, missiles and coffins. Novosibirsk artist Artem Loskutov has depicted a trunk of the birch tree by making black incisions on a white canvas using a police baton, a symbol of Russia's police state. I also loved Igor Ost's theatre curtain with the sign 'Past Continuous'.

The exhibition is spread over three rooms, one of which has faulty lighting. Some of the works are hung so high up that it's difficult to see them properly. Others are displayed on screens because it wasn't possible to bring them to Amsterdam. There is no one else here but me, despite the exhibition being free to enter. But none of that matters. It's the first time I have seen anything like this, and I'd like to think it's just the beginning. One picture, as they say, is worth a thousand words. One hundred pictures is a powerful display of dissent, solidarity and resistance.

None of these works could be displayed inside Russia today. Indeed, Philippenzo, one of the artists exhibited here, had to flee Moscow after his audacious piece caught the attention of Russian officials. On 12 June 2023, celebrated as Russia Day, Philippenzo unveiled his graffiti *ИЗРОССИЛОВАНИЕ* (*Izrossilovaniye*), a portmanteau of the Russian words for 'rape' and 'Russia'. The artist was detained for 'politically motivated vandalism', a criminal charge that carries up to three years in prison. He was released after a month, and later the police searched his flat, confiscating his works and devices. When ordered to return for further questioning, Philippenzo headed for the border and crossed first into Armenia and then Lithuania, where he now lives. Back in Russia, the Interior Ministry put him on the wanted list.

Philippenzo has also travelled to the Donetsk area of Ukraine and created graffiti depicting a field of makeshift Russian soldiers' graves topped with 'Z'-style crosses and surrounded by hogweed, a toxic plant. Another of his works displayed at De Balie is a TV set showing *Swan Lake*. The text above and below the set reads: 'We have been hoping to see the ballet for the twenty long years'. Originally, this artwork was graffiti, created by Philippenzo in Yekaterinburg in 2019. Putin had been in power for twenty years at that time. In the 1980s, Soviet TV used to broadcast *Swan Lake* during days of mourning after the deaths of Soviet leaders Brezhnev, Andropov and Chernenko. Most famously, *Swan*

Lake was shown on repeat during the August 1991 coup, which ultimately led to the break-up of the Soviet Union.

I call Philippenzo in Vilnius where he has been recuperating. It turns out that his shoulder joint was damaged during his arrest in Moscow, but alongside physical therapy, he is also trying to recover his mental health. 'Can you imagine legging it at short notice with nothing but a small rucksack?' I confess that I cannot.

'What is it like living in Vilnius?' I ask.

'Lithuania offers refuge for people from Russia, Belarus and Ukraine. European human rights and art organisations make it possible for people like me to settle down, get a sense of safety and security and get back to work.'

'Are you a political artist?'

'Not at all. I have a ton of ideas, and I want to realise them all. Back in Russia, I was responding to what was in front of me: fascism, police brutality and decay. Maybe here I'll start painting neo-pop art and female nudes.'

I'm almost disappointed to hear that. His works cleverly juxtapose words and images that cut through the epidemic of indifference inside Russia. Take ЦИНК НАШ! (*Zinc is ours!*), a sign written across rows of zinc coffins, a play on the slogan, 'Crimea is ours!' He painted it in his hometown, Volgograd, on 9 May 2022, when Russians traditionally commemorate the anniversary of victory in the Great Patriotic War. His piece was a reminder of the real costs of war, and it posed a question: should we still be celebrating victory when our country has turned into the invader?

'You are romanticising art,' he tells me. 'Art won't help persuade those who cannot be persuaded.'

'Do you miss Russia?'

'My Russia doesn't exist any more. It's falling apart. The people, the places – anything worth missing is gone. Take Moscow, for example. It's shining [from all the money being poured into it], it's buzzing, it's dancing. But it's turning into trash.'

We talk about what it means to be Russian. There are two words for it in our native language: one denotes Russian ethnicity, the other refers to being a citizen of the Russian Federation. Philippenzo says he does not recognise either meaning; to him, both are social constructs.

'On the other hand, Russian language and culture mean everything to me. I create using Russian words, I play with their meaning, I take them apart and make up new ones.'

I nod. Yes, only a Russian speaker would get *Izrossilovaniye* or even ВОЙНА – ЭТО ПОЗОР (*War Is Shameful*), where the artist has replaced the Cyrillic letter '3' with the Latin 'Z', the symbol of Putin's invasion in Ukraine.

I thank him for his art. Apart from speaking to my own soul, the works displayed in Amsterdam show people in Europe that many Russians stand against the regime and aren't afraid to show it.

'Завтра заперто на переучёт' is a line from a song, released in August 2024 by the founding father of Russian rock, Boris Grebenshchikov. It translates as 'Tomorrow is shut for taking stock' – a reference to days I remember from my childhood, when shops in the Soviet Union were sometimes closed to tally the inventory and the takings. As an idiom, 'taking stock' has the same meaning in English as in Russian, but perhaps only Russians would relate to their future being cancelled until we can figure things out.

'Is that the meaning?' I ask Grebenshchikov. I'm back in London, where I meet him for a coffee. He shrugs in response.

'I wrote the line – my work here is done. Now it's up to you to interpret it.'

The comments under his Instagram post suggest that this particular line of 'The Bad Song' resonates with many of his fans. I'm meeting 'BG', as he is often called, to see if music can help us process what is happening to our country and to understand the choices made by different contemporary Russian musicians. We start at the beginning.

Boris Grebenshchikov, who is seventy, was the founder and the lead singer of the St. Petersburg (then Leningrad) band Aquarium. They started performing in the 1970s, experimenting with folk and indie rock, pioneering the genres in the Soviet Union. Western music was officially banned at the time, and for the first decade or so, the band performed in friends' apartments with their music recorded on cassette tapes and passed on like samizdat books. Aquarium set the scene for new rock bands to form in the 1980s and 1990s, mostly in St. Petersburg and Yekaterinburg. I grew up with the music of Kino, Alisa, DDT, Chizh & Co, Nautilus Pompilius, Chaif and Zemfira.

'What was it like to perform under censorship in the Soviet Union? Do you feel a sense of déjà vu now?'

'Back then, the regime was getting tired. You would get a slap on the wrist, but you wouldn't get jailed. We didn't see the violence we witness now. A new broom sweeps clean.'

BG gave his last concert in Russia the day before the full-scale invasion of Ukraine. The world changed overnight. He caught the last Finnair flight out of St. Petersburg and returned to London, where he has lived permanently since 2019. Grebenshchikov was one of the first Russian musicians to speak out publicly: 'The war with Ukraine is madness. The people who started it brought shame on Russia.' In 2023, he was declared a 'foreign agent' in Russia, with official channels calling him a traitor. He hasn't been back since and is resigned to staying in exile: 'It wouldn't be very conducive to write from prison – I prefer to rent a studio in London,' he said in an interview in 2023.

I ask him about his fellow Russian rockers. Some have shown incredible bravery in criticising the Kremlin, like Yury Shevchuk of the rock band DDT, who, at a Russian concert in May 2022, declared, 'The motherland, my friends, is not the president's ass that has to be slobbered and kissed all the time. The motherland is an impoverished babushka at the train station selling potatoes.' He was interrogated, charged with discrediting the Russian Armed Forces and all his concerts in Russia were cancelled. Shevchuk continued his tour abroad, performing in Kazakhstan, Israel and Cyprus, and speaking out against the war and tyranny. His song 'Freedom' starts with the words, '[My] soul is disgusted by the indifference of the walls around [me].'

Others, like Vyacheslav Butusov, formerly of Nautilus Pompilius, and the rock band Chaif, both of whom emerged from my hometown in the 1980s, have sided with the Russian government and still give concerts in Russia, sometimes explicitly in support of the 'Special Military Operation'. Butusov has formed a new band, The Order of Glory, which performs his old catalogue. It feels like a betrayal that a band with a military name is performing songs that, at the dusk of the Soviet era, became synonymous with freedom. Chaif, which wrote many songs in the 1980s that helped Russians process the fates of young boys sent to fight in Afghanistan, has been performing at state events celebrating the 'reunification' with Crimea and the Donbas since 2014. The lead singer, Vladimir Shakhrin, even sent his guitar as a present to the Russian army battalion occupying the Kherson region of Ukraine. To me, it's bitterly disappointing.

'How could this be?' I ask BG.

'Some people simply want to belong, and they will always follow the crowd. And some people are motivated by money, and there is plenty of that in Moscow. These people would do anything, including shouting war slogans and waving Russian flags.'

'So you don't think they've changed?'

'No, they've just revealed themselves.' He speaks with sadness but without judgement.

'What about you? You are writing new music, translating Buddhist books and painting. What is your motivation? Is there a sense of responsibility to give us music that will cut through the propaganda?'

'It's not like that. A poet writes because he is called to do so. The creative force comes not from the outside, but from within. True art comes from the heart.'

I'm thinking the corollary must also be true. Art produced only for money, be it music or anything else, will never touch the soul.

'I hope you recognise that your songs help people in difficult times,' I tell him.

'If my music helps even just one person, I'm glad.'

'What about people back in Russia who have chosen "inner emigration" or who support the regime? How can they be reached?'

'I'm not sure they can be. You can offer someone a hand, but it's up to them to take it.'

And with that Grebenshchikov heads back to the recording studio.

*

It will come as no surprise that as a writer my biggest hope lies with literature. Books have the capacity to soothe and help process grief, and provide answers, purpose and meaning. Can the written word help us resuscitate our culture and build a different vision for Russia, one that we can be proud of someday?

In December 2023, Russian authorities put Boris Akunin on their list of 'extremists and terrorists'. Akunin rose to fame in the late 1990s as the author of historical detective novels and continued to write genre fiction, history books, plays and screenplays, essays and short stories. He is Russia's most widely read contemporary author. Akunin, who has lived in London for a decade, has been one of the most vocal critics of the war and the Kremlin among Russia's writers and artists. After the government announced his blacklisting, he commented on it on his blog:

> My ill-fated motherland is being run by criminals. The people who live there are their hostages, including those who don't realise this yet ... A seemingly minor event, the banning of books, some writer declared a terrorist, but in actual fact, it's an important milestone. Books have not been banned in Russia since the Soviet times. Writers have not been accused of terrorism since the Great Terror.

I couldn't think of a better person to help me with my quest than Akunin. He wrote an interesting post comparing Russia to an ice sheet that had split into two pieces, now rapidly moving away from one another. Talking about the arts, he described culture inside Russia as 'a censored, polished creature on all fours that knows how to wag its tail'. It's the type of culture Russia used to have in the Soviet days. 'There will emerge a counterculture born out of defiance, with its own secret language, books passed on to one another and writers living in Russia published under pen names abroad.'

In London, I ask him to start at the beginning and to recall how he felt in February 2022 after the full-scale invasion of Ukraine.

'At first, I had the distinct feeling that life as we knew it was over. What awaited us was going to be very different – and foul. I'm used to working on three books simultaneously, but I couldn't bring myself to write. It felt meaningless. I remember thinking "This is the end of Russia", and, of course, I was desperately worried about my Ukrainian friends.'

Fortunately, Akunin shook himself out of that stupor very quickly. A week later he and two friends, choreographer Mikhail Baryshnikov and economist Sergei Guriev, launched a charitable organisation, True Russia, which began fundraising from the Russian diaspora to help Ukrainian refugees. Theirs was one of the first such initiatives and raised about $1.5 million. Now, two and a half years later, Akunin believes that he should stick to his knitting.

'My area of expertise is literature – or culture, in a broader sense. I'm convinced that the fate of the war, the fate of Russia and the fate of all Eastern Europe depend on the sentiment coming from within Russia. The crisis won't be over for as long as ordinary Russians tolerate Putin,' explains Akunin. 'My purpose is to fight for their hearts and minds.'

Akunin teamed up with liked-minded authors, journalists and broadcasters to set up an online publishing platform, BAbook. Launched in 2024, it grew very quickly from a collection of his own e-books and musings into an umbrella platform that sells and promotes new books by Russian-speaking authors. Roskomnadzor, the Russian censor, took notice. They banned the BAbook website in Russia, which delighted the editorial board. Russian users are still accessing it using VPNs.

'This is our territory,' says Akunin with a smile. 'Here we are certainly stronger than Putin.'

In parallel to this online platform, Prague Book Tower, a Russian-language book fair, was launched in Prague in September 2024, coinciding with the fiftieth anniversary of the publication of Aleksandr Solzhenitsyn's *The Gulag Archipelago* in Paris. The fair, sponsored by Russian-language publishers based in France, Sweden, Germany, the Czech Republic, Israel and Canada, hosted book presentations, talks and discussions over the course of three days.

'This "publishing boom" is an interesting and promising movement,' says Akunin. Russians have always prided themselves in being "the literary people". The fact that they began banning books in Russia only increases their value. Recently, Roskomnadzor banned the little-known novel *Mouse* by Ivan Filippov. As a result, sales of *Mouse* at BAbook went through the roof.'

I remember seeing Yevgeny Roizman's books at the museum book shop in Yekaterinburg, wrapped in brown paper and labelled as content created by a 'foreign agent'. Russian books presented at the fair in Prague or displayed on the BAbook site are sending the opposite message: they are symbols of freedom of speech and self-expression in defiance of the Kremlin. Books are also a way to reclaim the Russian language. If dissident writers are silent, the language is owned by propaganda. Is it therefore our duty to speak up. I ask Akunin if he agrees.

'It depends on the writer. I am the author who has benefitted hugely from readers' generosity, even love. It would be shameful to hide in a hole. I have been on the receiving end for many years, and it is my time to give back. I use my public influence to do good, even if the price I have to pay is to be called "the enemy" in the Motherland.'

'And do you think you can make a difference?'

'Who knows, but at least I won't lose my own self-respect.'

Since both of us live in London, I ask him how Russian culture here in the West can help people see that Russia and Russians aren't one and the same.

'We need Western society to understand one thing only: there are two Russias. Think of the two heads of the eagle on the Russian coat of arms: one is looking to the East, the other to the West. One loves the idea of an empire, another loves freedom. The two heads have been fighting each other for the last two hundred years. And when the West – as happened in 2022 – decides that it's dealing with a single predatory pterodactyl that needs to be squashed and cancelled, Putin is jubilant. This attitude only strengthens his power. Russia isn't a pterodactyl – it's a phoenix. Help it rise from the ashes, don't stomp it out. Fight Putin's Russia, not Pushkin's.'

Browsing BAbook, a new work by Russian author Mikhail Shishkin caught my attention. Shishkin, who has lived in Switzerland since 1995, has written novels, short stories and essays in Russian, English and German. He has been openly criticising Putin's government since 2013, when he called on the West to boycott the 2014 Winter Olympics in Sochi. His new book is called *My Essays on Russian Literature* and starts with a question: 'What is wrong with the world created in Cyrillic?' Most of his essays focus on the purpose of literature: why do we need Tolstoy, Turgenev, Gogol and Chekhov if they failed to prevent the Gulag or the war with Ukraine? He starts with Pushkin.

Alexander Pushkin is not very well known to Western readers, probably because even Vladimir Nabokov's English translation of *Yevgeny Onegin*, his famous novel in verse, failed to do justice to the original Russian. But in Russia Pushkin is sacred. Not everyone in Russia has read the Bible or Koran, but every Russian can quote the beginning of *Yevgeny Onegin*. Shishkin argues that it was Pushkin who first took the European values of 'liberté, égalité, fraternité', which arrived in Russia in the mideighteenth century when Peter the Great 'hacked the window into Europe', and weaved them into poetry. As if echoing Boris Akunin, Shishkin writes:

> since those times Russia has had two types of people: they both speak Russian, but in two different languages. One head is filled with European education, liberal ideas and notions that Russia belongs to the global civilisation. This head doesn't want to wheedle; it wants freedom, rights and a constitution. The other head has its own view of the world: Russia is a special vessel making its own way in an ocean of enemies, and only its Captain in the Kremlin can lead it and keep it safe.

Shishkin writes that Pushkin's *Yevgeny Onegin* is not just a tale of an unhappy love, 'it is the first Russian text about the most important thing – human dignity'.

Since *Yevgeny Onegin* and Pushkin's other works endured when God himself was banned in the Soviet Union, it is perhaps true that, at least for Pushkin's Russians, their guiding principles do not come from the church or the TV screen – they come from within. Shishkin reminds us that, in the 1930s, when poet and novelist Boris Pasternak was told to sign a petition calling for 'enemies of the people' to be shot, and his pregnant wife begged him on her knees to comply for the sake of their unborn child, Pasternak replied that, if he signed the petition, he would become another person – and he didn't care about that person's child. In another example, Shishkin recalls August 1968, when eight Soviet citizens went to Red Square with banners, including some bearing the slogan 'For Your Freedom and Ours!', to protest against the invasion of Czechoslovakia. More recently, in 2024, Alexei Navalny held a card in court displaying these handwritten words: 'I am not afraid – don't you be afraid.' We have seen the same remarkable display of human dignity in all the available photos of the trials of Russian political prisoners: each one of them has held their head high, often forming a heart shape with their hands.

As I read Shishkin, I remind myself of Leo Tolstoy's anti-war activism and the groundbreaking investigative work by Anton Chekhov, who, despite suffering from tuberculosis, undertook an arduous journey to a penal colony on Sakhalin in the Far East of Russia, where he documented the brutal conditions of forced labour, disease and abuse, which was published as *Sakhalin Island* in 1895. Today, Russian readers especially, primarily think of Tolstoy as the author of epic novels and admire Chekhov for his timeless plays and short stories. And I wonder if praising classic Russian literature involves romanticising the past a little too much?

In 1933, Ivan Bunin was the first Russian writer to be awarded the Nobel Prize in Literature. To my shame, I had not read him until recently. I picked his most famous collection of short stories, *Dark Alleys*, and hoped to be transported into a world of love, romance and prose that reads like poetry. Bunin came from a noble family and discovered his talent at the age of seventeen, publishing his first poem. A friend of Chekhov and inspired by Tolstoy, he wrote one autobiographical novel, but he is most famous for his lyrical yet realistic short stories. In 1918, he left Moscow for Kyiv and then Odessa, where he became editor of the anti-Bolshevik newspaper *Rus*. In 1920, he boarded the last French ship out of Odessa and eventually settled in Paris. *Dark Alleys* is an achingly beautiful tribute to Russian nature, aristocratic country estates and the carefree innocence of young men in pre-revolutionary Russia. It is also full of outrageous stories where upper-class protagonists take advantage of village girls, who nevertheless fall in love with their assailants. In 'Styopa', a young merchant forces himself upon the daughter of an innkeeper. The girl curls up into a ball from the horror of her ordeal but still hopes the merchant will marry her. He promises her as much, but the next day he leaves for a fashionable resort in the Caucasus. This particular story was written in 1938 during the Great Terror in Russia. In fact, all of the *Dark Alleys* stories were written between 1937 and 1949, following unimaginable upheavals and horrors in Russia and the world at large. Bunin's prose is drenched in an old man's longing for 'his Russia', with its distinct seasons and crunchy apples, alongside his strange obsession with the 'round knees' of his muses and a pervasive sense of entitlement. A century later, I hope contemporary Russian émigré authors won't be wallowing in nostalgia. What we need is a path towards the 'Beautiful Russia of the Future'.

When Boris Akunin was declared an 'extremist and terrorist', no one inside Russia said a word. The silence coming from Russia after each new political charge, arrest and sentence is disheartening. Words can defeat silence. Writers in exile can be their megaphones. Contemporary writing can help us process the invasion and prepare us to make amends with Ukraine. But we need to dig deeper. Our values and our language need to change too.

Forward-thinking writers acknowledge that Russia cannot leap forwards without reconciling with its past. Like Britain, Russia needs to fall out of love with its imperial leanings. Shishkin writes, 'My Russia is a country that has freed itself from its *derzhava* boot.' 'Derzhava' means 'power' in the imperial sense, with the root of the word being 'to hold'.

We need to set our neighbours free, recognise their sovereignty and true independence, and then re-establish egalitarian relationships in Central Asia, the Caucasus and Eastern Europe. To achieve this, we must re-examine the dark passages of our history. The Russian language has to reform too. Many Russians still refer to Ukraine and other close countries as if they remained Soviet republics. Shameful derogatory words used to describe Ukrainians or people from the Caucasus still linger in the vocabulary. I've heard such words spoken by liberal Russians now living in London.

There's a famous phrase about eradicating the slave mentality ('to squeeze out a slave, drip by drip') belonging to Chekhov, who wrote about servility, sycophancy, deference and hypocrisy – or call it doublethink – as traits that reinforce the Russian false sense of esteem for the tsar. When I spent time in Russia, I heard this sentiment expressed a lot: 'Putin knows best.' I do not believe in these traits being inherited, but there is something about reverence to authority that many Russians cannot renounce. We have not had much time to practise democracy since *veche*, a people's assembly, was abolished in the sixteenth century by the central power of Moscow. It will take time to change the national mentality, and books have a role to play in showing us how.

My ultimate hope for the Russian language and culture is that they will unite us. Over the last two decades, the Kremlin has put a lot of effort into killing its political opponents. After the death of Navalny and the imprisonment and self-imposed exile of many other anti-government activists, it will take time to build a united opposition front. In the meantime, let artists bring us together in spirit. And as doctor Astrov says in *Uncle Vanya*: 'Those who will live a hundred or two hundred years after us, and who will despise us for how stupidly and tastelessly we have lived our lives, they will, perhaps, find a way to be happy . . .' Ah, Chekhov.

Chapter 11

The Good Russian

On 1 August 2024, Russia and the West conducted the largest prisoner swap since the Cold War. Thanks to complicated negotiations involving Germany, the US, Slovenia, Norway, Poland and Turkey, four Americans, five Germans and seven Russians (some with dual citizenship), were exchanged for some of Putin's hitmen, hackers and spies. Those imprisoned in Russia had been sentenced for 'extremism', 'treason' and 'discrediting the Russian army', including regional coordinators of Navalny's foundation Lilia Chanysheva, Ksenia Fadeeva and Vadim Ostanin; human rights activist Oleg Orlov; head of Mikhail Khodorkovsky's Open Russia, Andrei Pivovarov; artist Alexandra Skochilenko; journalist Alsu Kurmasheva; and opposition politicians Ilya Yashin and Vladimir Kara-Murza. Kara-Murza, a political activist, historian and protégé of the murdered Russian politician Boris Nemtsov, had been twice poisoned with nerve agent. Sentenced to twenty-five years for treason and having spent eleven months in solitary confinement, he was expected to die in prison due to his compromised health and harsh treatment. The Kremlin may have achieved their goal of repatriating assassins and secret agents, but it's the West who claimed the moral victory by freeing sixteen political prisoners and giving them their lives back.

While the Americans – journalist Evan Gershkovich, who was imprisoned for over a year on fabricated espionage charges; security executive and ex-US marine Paul Whelan; and Radio Liberty correspondent Alsu Kurmasheva – have understandably sought privacy to process and recuperate from their ordeal, Yashin, Kara-Murza and Pivovarov decided to host a press conference immediately after their release. The very next day, after a medical examination in a German hospital, they were sitting in a room full of journalists, thanking everyone involved in the negotiations and patiently answering questions. Wearing hastily purchased H&M clothes instead of their prison robes, they looked exactly as they said they felt – surreally happy and grateful to be free.

Two weeks later, Russian YouTube blogger Yury Dud released a three-hour interview with Ilya Yashin. Forty-one-year-old Yashin had been a colleague of both the late Nemtsov and Navalny. In 2017, he was elected as a municipal deputy of one of Moscow's districts. In the summer of 2022, after Yashin broadcast about the war crimes in Bucha to his YouTube audience, he was arrested and sentenced to eight and a half years for spreading false information about the Russian Armed Forces. Two years later he is sitting in a German studio, rented for the interview, looking remarkably well. It turns out that a famous barber, who used to cut hair of Moscow celebrities, was in the prison colony with Yashin. 'It was the best-looking colony in Russia,' he says, 'with both prisoners and their guards sporting trendy haircuts.' He shares interesting titbits about life in the colony: inmates keeping cats in their cells, prison censors being unexpectedly courteous with Yashin, probably because, after reading so many letters filled with love and admiration for him, they cannot help but think that he is a good person.

Watching the interview, I realised it was the first time since the invasion began in February 2022 that I had felt positive. The relief of seeing journalists and political prisoners free filled me with joy, and listening to Yashin, I could not help but be optimistic. For here was a Russian politician who appeared calm and composed, barely out of prison, but already with an action plan. Yashin said that he wanted to continue his work of talking to ordinary people about the war. He used to condemn the invasion from YouTube and via social media; in prison, he talked to other inmates, trying to dissuade them from joining the army in exchange for a pardon. Days after his release, he had already held a rally in Germany, speaking to two thousand Russians in exile. He said it was up to Ukraine to decide when to start negotiating for peace and on what terms. 'I have no moral right to tell Ukrainians what to do.' I was watching YouTube and nodding, as I imagine did millions of others. Within a fortnight, the video had nine million views.

Vladimir Kara-Murza was reunited with his wife and children in the US. In his interview with the US networks, he praised his wife, who had campaigned for his release. Kara-Murza, who looked thin and fragile, talked about the conditions of his solitary confinement in a penal colony in Omsk. He had a cot bed, which was bolted up against the wall from 5 a.m. until 9 p.m., meaning that during the day he could only pace around the cell or sit on a small, very uncomfortable stool. He was allowed to use pen and paper for only ninety minutes a day. Kara-Murza, who has a history degree from the University of Cambridge, expressed optimism that one day, when we least expect it, Putin's regime will collapse. It has happened in Russia before, with the end of the Romanov reign in 1917 and the dissolution of the Soviet Union in 1991. 'When this happens, we need to be ready,' said Kara-Murza, explaining that the Russian opposition would need to start working on 'a roadmap to transition Russia back towards democracy and reintegration into the civilised world.'

Both Yashin and Kara-Murza talked about working with other opposition politicians and activists, emphasising that there is a lot they can do together: condemning Russia's aggression in Ukraine, campaigning for the release of political prisoners in Russia and speaking on behalf of those ordinary people who oppose the regime but cannot do so themselves from inside Russia. It was a breath of fresh air. To put it in context, up to then the Russian opposition leaders in exile could not seem to agree on anything. Mikhail Khodorkovsky, Garry Kasparov, members of Alexei Navalny's Anti-Corruption Foundation and many other opposition activists and media personalities were constantly bickering on social media and had never found a way to get together and agree on an agenda. The fighting got worse after the death of Alexei Navalny, when his team were understandably angry and distraught – we all were. The Kremlin had eliminated its arch-enemy, the man who had inspired millions of Russians, even from behind bars, and his death crushed the hope some of us still clung to. Yulia Navalnaya's stoicism and defiance gave us some solace, but it was overshadowed by continuous squabbling. When both Yashin and Kara-Murza appeared so calm, composed and ready to collaborate, it felt like a ray of light piercing through the months of darkness.

One of their stated priorities was diplomacy and advocacy on behalf of political prisoners in Russia. Russian independent human rights group OVD-Info had recorded 1,109 anti-war criminal cases in Russia as of 12 December 2024. Half of the charges relate to the 'dissemination of fake information' or 'discreditation' of the Russian Armed Forces; 409 people have been accused of 'terrorism' or 'extremism'. Twenty-five people have been charged with treason, including dual Russian-US citizen Ksenia Karelina, who has been in custody since January 2024 and was sentenced by a court in Yekaterinburg to twelve years in jail two weeks after the first prisoner exchange. Her crime was to have donated $51.80 to a US-registered Ukrainian charity, Razom, at the beginning of the full-scale invasion while living in Los Angeles. Karelina was freed in a prisoner swap between Moscow and Washington in April 2025.

I have not seen my parents for nearly a year since my last visit. At the end of the summer, my mother sent me photos of mushrooms she had picked in the forest, reminding me of how much I loved her *gruzdi*, a type of mushroom commonly found in the Urals.[1] Traditionally, they are pickled and eaten as a side dish with thick sour cream. My mother fretted about the end of the gardening season: 'Who will be helping me tidy up the greenhouse this year?' I hummed something unhelpful in response. I had been talking to my mother about the fate of Ksenia Karelina for over six months by that point. It took that amount of time for it to sink in that I couldn't visit any more. It was simply too dangerous for someone like me, with dual Russian and British citizenship, to enter Russia. My mother struggled to believe that anything

---

1. *Lactarius resimus*

bad might happen to me in Russia, but Karelina's case helped her see the potential risks and accept my decision. It wasn't easy for either for us.

At about the same time, I went to see an exhibition called Brainwashing Machine that had arrived in London from Madrid. It was put together by the art group Anónimo; its members do not reveal their names, but they don't conceal their Russian roots. The exhibition in London was set up in an old crypt, cold and damp, even on a warm day. Inside there were artworks and interactive elements that painted a picture of Russia under Putin. Visitors were reminded that after Vladimir Putin became president in 2000, some independent media outlets were shut down and some acquired by the state or state-controlled enterprises. Censorship was established. Journalists were assassinated. In 2012, a 'foreign agent' law was introduced to label and restrict the activities of NGOs and other organisations who receive any funding from abroad. By 2022, anyone, including individuals, could be branded a 'foreign agent' for simply being deemed 'under foreign influence' by the state censor. As of 19 July 2024, the register of 'foreign agents' included 1,025 undesirable organisations and individuals, among them 309 media outlets (*Novaya Gazeta*, *Meduza*, TV Rain, Radio Liberty, *The Insider*, *The Moscow Times* and others), 82 human rights organisations (The Memorial; Golos, an independent election monitoring organisation; Nasiliu Net, an organisation helping victims of domestic violence), 41 environmental organisations and 46 musicians and artists.

Photographs of political prisoners, some as young as twenty-one and others in their thirties, forties, fifties and even sixties, smiling defiantly as they are sentenced in closed courts, have been pegged to a rope against a crumbling brick wall. Poets

Artem Kamardin and Egor Shtovba were sentenced to prison for seven and five and a half years respectively for reciting poems that protested the war and mobilisation in Moscow. Journalist Maria Ponomarenko from Barnaul in Western Siberia was given six years for sharing a post on Telegram about the bombing of the Drama Theatre in Mariupol. She has been repeatedly held in solitary confinement despite her deteriorating mental health. Artist Lyudmila Razumova and her husband Alexander Martynov from the Tver region painted 'Putler Kaput' and 'Ukraine, forgive us' on the walls of local shops and posted photos of their graffiti on social media. They were sentenced to seven and six and a half years in prison for vandalism and 'spreading false information' about the Russian army. Anastasia Dyudyaeva and her Ukrainian husband, Alexander Dotsenko, from a small town near St. Petersburg, left cards on supermarket shelves with the message 'Putin to the gallows' written in Ukrainian. They were sentenced to three and a half years for 'inciting terrorism'. Siberian artist Tatyana Laletina sent $10 to a Ukrainian fund in February 2022 and $20 two months later. She was given nine years for treason. Pianist Pavel Kushnir was arrested in May 2024 for posting anti-war videos on his YouTube channel, which had five subscribers. He went on a hunger strike and died in a pre-trial detention centre two months later.

English translations of some of the denunciation letters are displayed in a ring binder. A group of thirteen- and fourteen-year-old schoolchildren from Penza reported their English and German teacher to the authorities after she told them that Ukraine was an independent country and Russia was a totalitarian state. Irina Gen was summoned for questioning by the FSB, where she discovered the children had filmed her. She was given a three-year suspended sentence and barred from teaching during that time. Famously, the artist Sasha Skochilenko, who had replaced supermarket price tags with facts about the war in Ukraine, was informed on by a fellow citizen. The 'Important Stories' Telegram channel estimated that in the two and a half years since February 2022, some 3,500 complaints were made via vigilante Telegram channels specialising in anti-Russia, anti-war or pro-LGBT+ rhetoric. Members of the channel 'Mrakoborets' ('Fighter of Darkness') have been especially prolific, reporting on citizens around three times a day. Anthropologist Alexandra Arkhipova wrote about one self-proclaimed 'professional unpaid snitch' who had informed on 764 people, including Arkhipova herself, during the first year after the full-scale invasion. The informer studied the YouTube channels of media platforms banned in Russia and reported on people who gave interviews to TV Rain or the BBC. Their motivation was to help shut down TV Rain, which, by their reasoning, would struggle to find people to interview, wouldn't have anything to report on and therefore wouldn't be able to attract paying subscribers. Arkhipova got in touch with the informer, which is how she learned about the scale of their activities.

After studying the photographs and letters of denunciation I got to two of my favourite pieces in the exhibition. One was a voting table with two options: 'Publicly express an opinion and risk going to jail' or 'Stay at home and tolerate the unfairness'. I was amused to see that both transparent urns contained an equal number of tokens. Idealistic voting decisions are certainly easy to make from the safety of London. My second favourite exhibit was a spinning wheel. The rules are simple: express your opinion while inside the Brainwashing Machine and try your luck. I did. As the wheel was spinning, I skimmed the options:

1. This time you get off lightly
2. Just a couple of bruises
3. Pay the fine
4. Prison
5. You are now under a travel ban
6. You are now a foreign agent
7. You've just lost your job
8. Smile! You are on a federal wanted list!
9. You've been declared a terrorist and an extremist
10. Welcome to the pre-trial detention centre!

The arrow pointed at 4. The chill of the crypt suddenly got to me, and I rushed to get out. The traffic hummed contentedly on a busy London road. Mothers with buggies strolled past me. I squinted from the sun and thought what a luxury that was.

I began working on this book with a title – one that I have yet to tackle head on. Who is 'The Good Russian'? Does one even exist? Perhaps I have been avoiding these questions because there are no good answers. My trip to Russia in autumn 2023 – when I tried to be open-minded, listen to people of all persuasions and observe their way of life – made me see that black-and-white thinking would never help us understand each other or resolve any conflict. It was exasperating, to be sure, to talk to a paediatrician who treats sick children whose fathers have been lost to the senseless war with Ukraine yet still supports the Kremlin, believing that Russia is fighting to defend itself from NATO. It was difficult to see various members of my family and talk to them about anything but politics. Chapter after chapter, I have delved further into the impossible circumstances and desperate situations Russians have found themselves in, where the people who trusted me with their stories simply wanted to be heard.

In the end, I came to believe that the 'Good' in my title is a false idol. It was Vassily Grossman who came to question the concept in his twentieth-century masterpiece, *Life and Fate*. He wrote that the definition of 'good', as opposed to 'evil', always depends on the ideology of the person or the regime. To Putin and his followers, 'good' is sending troops to Ukraine, annexing its territories and toppling its government. 'Good' is interfering with elections in the West, with Russia flexing its muscles and playing the 2.0 version of the Cold War. 'Good' is instilling fear as a way to gain respect. An even better example of this relativism is the word 'patriotism'. In Putin's Russia, patriotism is what boys and girls are now being taught at school: your duty is to take up arms and breed future soldiers. And as my father said to me, 'It is your duty to return to your Motherland and serve the state.' But to me, and to many people like me, patriotism is the late politician Boris Nemtsov leading a rally in Moscow against the annexation of Crimea in 2014; the late journalist Anna Politkovskaya doggedly reporting from Chechnya despite repeated threats and intimidation before she was finally assassinated; investigators uncovering the state of corruption among the Kremlin elites; brave citizens covering walls with anti-war graffiti; and people inside Russia collaborating with independent news media outlets to tell the truth about what's happening. And politicians like Alexei Navalny, who returned to Russia after an attempt on his life by the Kremlin, and Vladimir Kara-Murza and Ilya Yashin, who openly condemned the invasion of Ukraine from inside Russia, are in a league of their own. In Putinspeak, they are traitors. To me, they are heroes and martyrs.

Grossman suggests that true, undisputed goodness is, in fact, kindness. It's in the everyday acts of ordinary people: prison guards showing mercy, civilians caring for wounded enemy soldiers, strangers sharing crumbs of bread with each other. With Grossman's words on my mind, I refrained from judging people based on their ideology and instead paid attention to their acts of compassion and kindness, however small. I saw plenty of that. The trouble is that a grave malaise seems to have taken hold of people in Putin's Russia. It can only be described as a callusing of the heart. When Ksenia Karelina was charged with high treason and sentenced to twelve years in a penal colony, no one came to protest her sentence; few media channels reported it. My mother nodded grimly when I called her on video. A friend in Russia commented, 'Well, what did you expect?' It's as if lawlessness has become such a staple in Russia that nothing shocks or touches people any more. Indeed, Russian Telegram channels and regional online media platforms are filled with worse crimes, such as rape and murder. In August 2024, a member of the armed forces fighting in Ukraine came home to Bogdanovich, a town near Yekaterinburg, and shot his ex-wife and her partner. There are many more such stories, often involving ex-convicts who were pardoned for enlisting in the army. The federal state-owned TV channels do not mention this epidemic. People don't talk about it either. Violence, too, it seems, has become normalised.

If the word 'Good' is tricky, then 'Russian' is even more complicated. I feel less like a citizen of the current Russian Federation, but I will always be Russian by birth. Is it something to shout about? And what does it mean when you are removed from your homeland? Is it even important to people like me, who live in cities like London and have long embraced global citizenship?

I remember Kostya and Sveta telling me that their gifted

daughter, Nadya, had found it impossibly hard to process Russia's aggression. A young tennis player competing in international tournaments, she was very much affected by the invasion and its aftermath. Even I found it difficult to say I was Russian when someone asked me, 'Where are you from?' Ultimately, I recovered and so did Nadya. The ability to relate to one's nationality in difficult times is linked to the concept of 'collective responsibility' that many of us have grappled with since the full-scale invasion of Ukraine.

'Collective responsibility' is a problematic concept coined in the twentieth century off the back of the atrocities committed by Nazi Germany and the Soviet Red Terror. It means that individual members of a community should be held accountable for the crimes committed by that community and face consequences.

Sergey Radchenko, a native of Sakhalin Island in Russia and professor at John Hopkins University, writes that both the Communists and Nazis assigned collective responsibility to whole categories of people.

Stalin unleashed the Holodomor and ordered the murder or mass deportation of the Poles, the Balts, the Chechens, the Crimean Tartars and the Koreans (among others). Hitler targeted the Jews and the Roma communities as well as homosexuals and other collective categories. Stalin exterminated entire 'classes' of people (such as rich peasants), a practice later adopted by other genocidal tyrants, not least Mao Zedong and Pol Pot.

After the Germans were assigned collective responsibility for genocide and the Second World War, they were expelled en masse from territories that Germany had lost in defeat.

This dubious lineage of collective responsibility, argues Radchenko, can be extrapolated using further examples:

> Let's argue for just a second that all Americans are 'collectively' responsible for the Vietnam War or the war in Iraq. The argument is jarring not only because many Americans were against both wars and actively opposed them, but also because there were other, non-American actors who were equally responsible for these conflicts, whether Communist radicals or Saddam's henchmen.

He continues, saying that, unlike in democratic societies, where one can plausibly argue in favour of collective responsibility based on free and fair elections, it's not the same for states like Putin's Russia, which has not had a free and fair election in decades. To those people who argue that ordinary Russians could do more to protest against the war or sabotage state plans, Radchenko offers a litmus test: 'The minimum threshold for pontificating on the virtues of opposing tyrants should be a proven record of a first-hand encounter with a police baton on the back and a kick in the teeth.'

The responsibility for the annexation of Crimea and the full-scale invasion of Ukraine must lie with the individual decision-makers: those who gave the orders, orchestrated them and carried them out. And Western governments and organisations should continue targeting Putin's officials and their enablers, including bankers and lawyers in the West who help launder the money of Russian government ministers, war financiers and propagandists. No one is under the illusion that it takes only one despot to carry out these crimes.

What worries me more than collective responsibility is the

dispersion of Russians in exile. Some people, like me, emigrated many years ago, while some Russians have left their homeland during the current war with Ukraine. We have all been primarily focusing on settling down, making new nests, finding jobs and striving to belong. It's a tale well known to any immigrant – the delicate balance of adopting a new way of life while simultaneously holding on to the customs and traditions you grew up with. It *is* possible, many even thrive, but you never really feel at home. When I spoke to new Russian migrants, they mostly talked about setting up their lives, the difficulties their kids were having in new schools, finding new friends, grocery prices and sourcing a brand of mayonnaise that 'tastes like home' to dress traditional Russian dishes, such as 'Herring Under a Fur Coat'. One friend said her children couldn't think of anything to be proud of about being Russian. While previously we could boast of Gagarin, Rostropovich and too many Nobel Prize winners in physics to count, today we have a dearth of Russian role models, other than those who end up in prison or dead. 'Martyrdom is not what I want to teach to my children.' Another friend, who has lived in Europe since 2021, confessed that if she never read another novel in Russian or went to a concert of Russian music again, it wouldn't matter to her in the slightest. 'I care about my family and how we get on. I can't say that I think much about being Russian in my everyday life.' Both sentiments are understandable, but in time I hope that a flourishing contemporary Russian culture, with new books, plays and films, will help pull us together. At the end of the day, we have a responsibility, being here in the West where we can express ourselves freely, to demonstrate that Russia isn't Putin. We cannot do that without some collective sense of belonging.

*

Last year, when I visited Stella, who had left Russia for Spain, we called our friend Vera back in Yekaterinburg. Vera was keen to learn how Stella had settled in Spain and how her children were getting on at school. 'Have they made any friends? Are they being bullied? Is Spanish education any good? How do they manage in their tiny new flat?' Back in Yekaterinburg, Misha and Vera are anxious about their twins' future. Stella's children now have a world of opportunities open to them in Europe. Once they overcome the initial difficulties, they'll be grateful to their parents for the future they gave them. I detected a certain tension in my friends' conversation and probed it further in the months that followed.

For those liberal Russians who decided to take the plunge and move abroad, they left behind their ageing parents, comfortable homes and stability, if not certainty over the future. They faced many obstacles in their new homes, from opening bank accounts and supporting their kids as they adjusted to new schools to experimenting with new local ingredients to satisfy fussy eaters. They engage in local events and try to embrace their new lives. Unrestricted in their access to the media, they read news about Russia every day, deliberately or subconsciously seeking validation for their decision. Those liberal Russians who stayed have their reasons to do so. For most people these are financial restrictions, language barriers, jobs they cannot do abroad, family members they must look after or simply preferring their own milieu. Many would agree it unimaginable to take off and start a new life in a foreign country without fluent command of the language or a strong sense of direction and belonging.

People like Vera and Misha took time to consider their options and made a conscious choice to stay in Russia. Their choice came with a whole list of compromises: they cannot say what they think, they can only access independent media sources via VPN and they must make peace with cognitive dissonance, restricted travel, censorship and limited opportunities for their children. Perhaps most poignantly, they realise that things are unlikely to get better in their lifetime. The tension I detected between Stella and Vera arose from the deeply buried yet ever-present question: have I made the right choice?

The rift between those who left and those who stayed is too painful to accept. Russians have already been polarised enough by the state's methodical propaganda, culminating in the creation of two camps: 'us' and 'them'. The Kremlin began using terms like 'fifth column', 'traitors', 'enemies of the state' in the 2010s, and they promptly made their way into the vocabulary of TV-watching Russians, including my father. It was inevitable that the war with Ukraine would cement the division into 'ours' and 'theirs' when talking about views, values or beliefs. In her book *The Future is History*, journalist Masha Gessen writes that news and talk shows on Russian TV have been deliberately designed to maintain a constant pitch of anxiety. The threat always came from the West, be it NATO, paedophiles or recreational drugs. Only 'strongman' Putin, protecting Mother Russia from enemy influence and uniting its people through common victories – such as the 'reunification' with Crimea – could provide some respite. Western scarecrows and manufactured paranoia inside Russia ensured apathy. 'There is nothing we can do but to pray and hope for the best,' my mother once said to me. This isn't genetic – it's learned behaviour. Russia 2024 is *Nineteen Eighty-Four* on steroids.

I do not have a precise map to find a way out and heal Russia as a nation, but I know that we cannot afford any rifts between those of us who think of war as a crime and freedom as an ideal to strive for. Whether we live in Russia or abroad, we must stick together. We have independent media resources like TV Rain, *Meduza*, *Novaya Gazeta* and *The Insider* to keep us informed; we have books, YouTube shows and music to fuel our souls and we have Russian, the language of uncensored discussions at the kitchen tables. When I asked a Russian friend who had lived in Essex for about a decade, 'What does it mean to be Russian when removed from our homeland?' he gave me an answer that made me close my laptop and head out to a small shop in North London.

When I first came to Britain, my palate was accosted by many strange foods, textures and flavours, like Marmite, mushy Weetabix cereal, salt and vinegar crisps and buttered baguettes filled with chips. Luckily, living in London meant being exposed to a wide variety of cuisines within an ever-evolving restaurant scene – probably the world's best. This meant that I have not been making Russian food or frequenting Russian restaurants in London. I have, however, savoured home cooking when back in Russia to see my family. During my last trip, my mother made a special effort, preparing all my favourite traditional dishes, as for once I was staying over for the entire month. Together we made *pelmeni* (meat dumplings) and tomato and horseradish sauce, pulling the roots from the vegetable patch before the frost arrived. My mother made *ukha*, a traditional fish soup, and *blini* – not the tiny blobs sold in UK supermarkets, but a stack of thin, buttery crêpes. There was *kholodets*, jellied beef stew; 'Olivier', a filling salad of boiled eggs, vegetables and ham; *borsh*, without the 't', served with thick soured cream; and 'Herring Under a Fur Coat', probably the most bizarre traditional Russian dish of all. Later, back in London, it became apparent that a trip to sample my mother's food may not happen again for a while. And so, when my friend replied that the necessary ingredient for maintaining a sense of Russianness in exile was to cook traditional dishes, I felt a strong craving. I texted my friends on the way to a Latvian grocery store and invited them over for dinner the next day: 'I hope you are feeling adventurous.'

'Herring Under a Fur Coat' combines the staple ingredients of modern Russian cuisine: boiled eggs, potatoes, carrots and beetroot; and pickled herring with onions and mayonnaise. Sourcing the latter ingredients is what food forums are for: you will find recipes transforming Hellman's into a Soviet staple and a ton of reviews of Polish, Latvian and Lithuanian brands available from specialist shops. The right herring isn't sold at a standard British supermarket either and must be tracked down. I once saw a newly emigrated Russian child in Amsterdam eating pickled Dutch herring straight from the jar. He'd be forlorn in London. Once I got my groceries, I video-called my mother to consult on the exact proportions of the ingredients and the order of the layers: it's herring on top of potatoes, followed by onions, carrots, eggs and finally beetroot, with each level generously smothered with mayonnaise. My mother had no faith: 'Your English friends won't touch it,' she said. I mentioned that a Scot and an Australian were coming too. She shook her head in dismay. As it happened, my friends admired the bright maroon centrepiece that I had set overnight. I expected them to be polite about it, but it was gone in two helpings. My mother couldn't believe it. Neither could I.

I once got into a conversation with a man sitting next to me on a plane when returning to London from Baku. He was an Iranian Azerbaijani who had fled Iran with his family after the 1979 Iranian Revolution and sought asylum in the UK. Some four decades later, they had planned a family trip to Azerbaijan and stayed in the area close to the border with Iran. He said that he saw the same trees and smelled the same mountain air that he remembered from his childhood. He was also able to speak Azerbaijani, a language he had nearly forgotten after speaking only Persian and English in the UK. His grown-up children were engrossed in videos on their iPads, so we kept on talking. He was wistful, saying it had been the trip of a lifetime. It made me think of Russian immigrants in context. Iranians left their homeland as families, which was undoubtedly traumatic, but it meant that they have been able to preserve their language, cuisine and culture more successfully than will be possible for the young Russian professionals who have left their homeland in haste, often leaving families behind. What is true for both Iranians and Russians is that no one expected the oppressive rule over their homelands to last for as long as it has.

Political scientist Alexander Morozov wrote that during his youth in the seventies and the eighties before perestroika, it felt like Stalinism was in the distant past. I'm sure my parents would agree with that sentiment. Now, in the 2020s, Morozov looks back through a different lens. Stalinism was formed during the three decades of his reign, from 1924 to 1953. Over the next three decades, Russia experienced a 'thaw' under Khruschev, a period of 'stagnation' under Brezhnev, Andropov and Chernenko, and a period of détente with the Helsinki Accords, but also a protracted war in Afghanistan.

This thirty-year era of post-Stalinist convulsions was a poorly executed attempt to remove the body of an elephant from a tiny studio flat. It gives you an idea of how long it might take to remove another 'elephant' after Putin.

New generations born to Russians in exile might want to visit their parents' homeland out of curiosity, but will they choose to move to Russia once the authoritarian regime there falls? Will they be motivated to build 'the beautiful Russia of the future'? I don't think so. It is therefore up to us, my generation, to do the work required to 'remove the elephant' and make space for a very different Russia. For that, we need to not just stay close to the liberal Russians who still live there, but also find a way to reconcile with 'the silent majority' who actively support Putin today. There is so much work to do. We must begin by finding common ground, and then a way to make peace with ourselves, our neighbours and the West.

We must reclaim Russia. I trust Kara-Murza, Navalnaya, Yashin and other like-minded politicians to work on ending the war on Ukraine's terms, returning occupied territories and planning reparations for Ukraine. I trust them to redraft the Russian Constitution and laws to steer the country towards genuine democracy. I hope that historians, social scientists and future political leaders will help us re-examine the Soviet and post-Soviet period, so that we can process Stalinism and Putinism in a way that ensures the generations who follow us won't have to learn their lessons the hard way by re-living them. I hope we can follow Germany's example of reconciliation, even though we have different wounds and ailments, which will take their own time and methods to heal. Living in Britain, I'm also thinking about its 'imperial syndrome' and the time and effort it is taking to review the country's colonial past and make amends as a nation. Russia, too, must re-think its Soviet legacy in relation to its neighbours – this is work that has not even begun. The xenophobia in Russia today, especially towards migrants from Central Asia, is abhorrent. We have never learned to treat our neighbours as independent sovereign states or admitted to the atrocities committed by the Soviet government in virtually every region of the USSR, including Georgia, Ukraine, Belarus and the Baltics. If we had, Russia would not have invaded Ukraine.

In August 2024, my father was diagnosed with brain cancer shortly after his seventieth birthday. A healthy and fit person throughout his life, he was shaken by the diagnosis. So was I. We have not really spoken since I had returned to London, but I called him at once when I heard the news. He said he wanted me to 'come home'. As an only child, I understood only too well that both of my parents needed me, for practical help and emotional support. For the first time since leaving Russia I was facing a very real dilemma: could I risk going to Yekaterinburg again? The arrests and sentencing of Alsu Kurmasheva (freed in August 2024), Antonina Favorskaya, Konstantin Gabov, Sergei Karelin, Artem Kriger and other journalists; and the imprisonment and the subsequent exchange of Ksenia Karelina, an ordinary woman who got a twelve-year sentence for making a modest charity donation in support of Ukraine, made it clear to me that travelling to Russia after February 2022 was a game of Russian roulette. I have already spun the cylinder twice. The odds of an outspoken dual Russian–British citizen getting detained had risen too high. I told my father I wouldn't be coming. He called me selfish and hung up the phone. In the days that followed I ruminated over the decisions I had made. Like hundreds of thousands of Russians who live in the West and still travel to Russia to see their families, I could have been more pragmatic and kept quiet. I could have put my family above everything else. But I didn't.

In time, my father came round a little, and we were able to speak over the phone. We tried to cast politics aside, but we couldn't find any common ground. In most conversations, he ended up talking about Russia's unique path, Putin standing up to the West and Russian soldiers defending the country's interests in Ukraine. He regretted that due to his age and ill health he couldn't be there himself. He talked about his father and the hardship his exiled family had endured. At the same time, my father told me how he admired Stalin for his mobilisation of the country to defeat Hitler and to industrialise the USSR. I listened and bit my tongue. It was a rift impossible to bridge. I was losing my father to cancer, but in truth, I had been losing him all along, drip by drip, over twenty-five years of Russia under Putin. He and I had chosen different visions of Russia. In the end, I have no choice but to accept it.

References

Epigraph

'A Piece of Advice from the Soviet Time: Do Not Be Afraid' – Interview with a Poet and Essayist, Lev Rubinstein on Poetry in the Era of Bucha, on the Death of Tyrants and Hope for the Best', *Meduza,* 7 January 2023 («Из времен СССР совет могу дать простой: не надо бояться» Интервью поэта и эссеиста Льва Рубинштейна — о поэзии в эпоху Бучи, смерти тиранов и надежде на лучшее)

Chapter 2: Doublethink

Sam Fleming and Daria Mosolova, 'West Probes Potential Sanction Dodging as Exports to Russia's Neighbours Surge', *Financial Times*, 23 February 2023.

Polina Ivanova and Chris Cook, 'Armenia: On the New Silk Road for Goods to Sanctions-Hit Russia', *Financial Times*, 18 July 2023.

Nestlé, 'Nestlé's Statement on Ukraine and Russia', obtained in December 2024, https://www.nestle.com/ask-nestle/our-company/answers/update-ukraine-russia.

Chapter 3: Life Goes On

Vladimir Putin, 'Address to the Nation', 24 February 2022, http://en.kremlin.ru/events/president/news/67843.

BBC, 'Russia's Losses in Ukraine', sourced on 18 October 2024, https://www.bbc.com/russian/articles/c5ywndyjjxoo.

Chapter 4: Churchill's Key

Natalia Dubtsova, 'From Pulpit to Propaganda Machine: Tracing the Russian Orthodox Church's Role in Putin's War', Reuters Institute for the Study of Journalism, University of Oxford, 6 February 2024, https:// reutersinstitute.politics.ox.ac.uk/pulpit-propaganda-machine-tracing-russian-orthodox-churchs-role-putins-war.

'Background on Bylinas in the Soviet Union', https://arzamas.academy/ materials/572.

'Bylinas in Contemporary Russia', https://www.svoboda.org/a/26723150.html.

Chapter 5: 'I Only Scream When I'm Asleep'

Institute for Study of Childhood, Family and Parenting of the Russian Federation, 'Curriculum for Important Conversations', obtained in January 2024, https://razgovor.edsoo.ru.

Chapter 6: Suspended hope

Website of the Roizman Foundation: https://roizmanfond.ru.

'Strong City. Yevgeny Roizman and Other Citizens of Yekaterinburg', ('Сильный город. Евгений Ройзман и другие жители Екатеринбурга') 21 August 2022, https://www.svoboda.org/a/royzman-i-drugie-zhiteli-ekaterinburga/31997151.html.

Katerina Gordeeva's interview with Yevgeny Roizman, https://www. youtube.com/watch?v=iRJfQ-YEcdU.

Chapter 7: 'Crimea is ours! And are *you* ours?'

Vladimir Putin, 'Address to the State Duma on Crimea', 18 March 2014, http://en.kremlin.ru/events/president/news/20603.

Arkady Ostrovsky, *The Invention of Russia* (Atlantic Books, 2015).

Dan Ariely, *Misbelief* (Heligo Books, 2023).

Svetlana Sosnovskikh, 'A. V. Bakunin on Repressions Within the System of Soviet Totalitarianism' ('А. В. Бакунин о месте репрессий в системе советского тоталитаризма'), (2007), obtained from the electronic archive of the Ural Federal University, https://elar.urfu.ru/ bitstream/10995/39468/1/uibch_2007_02_65.pdf.

Alexander Bakunin Remembered ('Александр Васильевич Бакунин в Воспоминаниях и Документах'), (AMB, 2004).

The Teacher and His School ('Учитель и Его Школа'), (UMTs-UPI, 2015).

Chapter 8: 'I couldn't live there any more'

Vasily Sukhomlinsky, 'A Book on Conscience', *Alphabet of Faith*, https://azbyka.ru/deti/kniga-o-sovesti-chast-1-krasota-radost-zhizni-chelovek-eto-sila-duha-suhomlinskij.

Alexei Navalny, 'Address to Supporters', 19 January 2021, https://www.bbc.co.uk/news/world-europe-55700312.

Chapter 9: The Accidentals

The Bell, 'After the Start of the War, About 650,000 People Left Russia and Never Came Back – A Study' ('После начала войны из России уехали и не вернулись около 650 тысяч человек: исследование'), 16 July 2024, https://thebell.io/posle-nachala-voyny-iz-rossii-uekhali-i-ne-vernulis-bolshe-700-tysyach-chelovek-issledovanie-the-bel.

On Georgia:

Joshua Kucera, 'After a Frosty Reception, Tbilisi's Wartime Russians Are Beginning to Leave', *Radio Free Europe / Radio Liberty*, 24 January 2024, https://www.rferl.org/a/georgia-russians-fleeing-war-leaving-/32784835.html.

International Republican Institute, *Georgian Survey of Public Opinion | September – October 2023*, published 15 November 2023, https://www.iri.org/resources/georgian-survey-of-public-opinion-september-october-2023/.

Tornike Chumburidze and Sofia Gavrilova, 'Russian Immigration to Georgia Sparks Tensions Ahead of Election', *Carnegie Politika*, 19 December 2023, https://carnegieendowment.org/russia-eurasia/politika/2023/12/russian-immigration-to-georgia-sparks-tensions-ahead-of-election?lang=en.

David Gormezano, 'In Georgia, Russian Émigrés See Familiar Kremlin Tactics', *France 24*, 16 May 2024, https://www.france24.com/en/europe/20240516-in-georgia-russian-émigrés-see-familiar-kremlin-tactics.

On Georgia and Armenia:

Tsypylma Darieva, 'Migration from Russia to Georgia and Armenia', *bbp: Bundeszentrale für politische Bildung*, 2 July 2024, https://www.bpb.de/themen/migration-integration/regionalprofile/english-version-country-profiles/550062/migration-from-russia-to-georgia-and-armenia/#footnote-target-11.

On Georgia and Kazakhstan:

Mariam Darchiashvili, Ketevan Gurchiani, Nikita Mishakov, and Caress Schenk, 'Local Responses to Russian Migration in Georgia and Kazakhstan', *PONARS Eurasia*, 29 May 2024, https://www.ponarseurasia.org/local-responses-to-russian-migration-in-georgia-and-kazakhstan/.

On 'Russophobia':

UK Government, 'UK Addresses Security Council Meeting on "Russophobia"', 14 March 2023, https://www.gov.uk/government/speeches/uk-addresses-security-council-meeting-on-russophobia-uk at the-un.

Chapter 10: Cancel Putin not Pushkin

Mark Wigglesworth, 'Mark's notes on Shostakovich Symphony No. 4', https://www.markwigglesworth.com/notes/marks-notes-on-shostakovich-symphony-no-4/

Alex Ross, 'Valery Gergiev and the Nightmare of Music Under Putin', *New Yorker*, 3 March 2022, https://www.newyorker.com/culture/cultural-comment/valery-gergiev-and-the-nightmare-of-music-under-putin.

Alec Russell, 'Ukrainian Author Oleksandr Mykhed: "We Do Not Know How Much Time We Have"', *Financial Times*, 10 July 2024, https://www.ft.com/content/9dbec3b4-6b98-4e55-9174-342069606563.

Andrew Roth, 'Russian Court Orders Closure of Country's Oldest Human Rights Group', *The Guardian*, 28 December 2021, https://www.theguardian.com/world/2021/dec/28/russian-court-memorial-human-rights-group-closure.

Boris Akunin, 'Comments on Being Declared a Terrorist', 18 December 2023, https://babook.org/posts/584.

Mikhail Shishkin, *My Essays on Russian Literature* ('Мои Эссе о Русской Литературе'), (BaBook, 2024).

Ivan Bunin, *Dark Alleys* ('Темные Аллеи'), (Азбука Классика, 2011).

Anton Chekhov, *Uncle Vanya*, act 4 (1897)

Chapter 11: The Good Russian

OVD-Info, 'Reports on Repressions and Political Prisoners in Russia', data obtained in December 2024, https://antiwar.ovd.info.

'On Snitches in Contemporary Russia', https://t.me/istories_media/6739.

Alexandra Arkhipova, 'Interview on Snitches', 26 May 2024, *Echo FM*, https://echofm.online/programs/chestno-govorya/chestno-govorya-s-aleksandroj-arhipovoj-u-etih-repressij-net-granicz.

Sergey Radchenko, 'Collective Responsibility and the Slide Into the Totalitarian Past', *The Moscow Times*, 15 August 2022, https://www.themoscowtimes.com/2022/08/15/collective-responsibility-a78572.

Masha Gessen, *The Future Is History: How Totalitarianism Reclaimed Russia* (Granta, 2017).

Alexander Morozov, Facebook, 21 November 2023, https://www.facebook.com/share/p/1ABHsXeQbe/

Acknowledgements

The idea for this book was born in June 2023 at the Dalkey Book Festival in Ireland, probably the best literary festival in the world. The brilliant *FT* columnist, Simon Kuper, heard me introduce myself as a 'good Russian' in jest and said it should be the title of my next book. I wrote a proposal for it in September that year and travelled to Russia straight after. Simon has been incredibly supportive throughout this book journey – I am very privileged to have such a generous colleague and friend.

I owe the greatest debt of gratitude to all the Russians who contributed to this book. They showed tremendous trust in me and this project. Quite simply, there wouldn't be a book without all the characters who spoke to me with so much candour. I sincerely hope I've done it justice and let these brave Russians be heard.

Elliot Prior and Rachel Goldblatt at Curtis Brown believed in this book from the outset. It was such a pleasure to work with these two super smart and talented agents who helped shape the idea of *The Good Russian* into a story. Thanks to them I met Sameer Rahim at The Bridge Street Press, an imprint of Little, Brown. I could not have imagined a better partner, whose acute vision, attention to detail, continuous encouragement and bril-liant editing helped sculpt the story into a book.

A special thank you goes to Jane Simpson and 'Stella', who read and edited early drafts and believed in me from day one. Writing is a lonely journey, but I have always had their love and support.

Thank you to Nithya Rae, Chevonne Elbourne and Zoe Hood at Little, Brown, and Peter Jacobs.

Thank you to all my clients – Ella Tyler, Leanne Linacre, Alex Cowan-Sanluis and Bonnie Chiu – who gave me opportunities for paid work and thereby supported this book. Any creative process requires some sense of security; it would not have been possible to write without an income to support myself.

Finally, thank YOU for buying this book. It means the world to me and many good Russians.

Index